Pastoral Care with Adolescents in Crisis

Books by G. Wade Rowatt, Jr.
Published by Westminster / John Knox Press

Pastoral Care with Adolescents in Crisis

with Mary Jo Rowatt

The Two-Career Marriage (Christian Care Books)

Pastoral Care with Adolescents in Crisis

G. Wade Rowatt, Jr.

Westminster/John Knox Press
Louisville; Kentucky

Book design by Gene Harris

First edition

Published by Westminster / John Knox Press
Louisville, Kentucky

PRINTED IN THE UNITED STATES OF AMERICA

9 8 7 6 5 4 3 2 1

Library of Congress Cataloging-in-Publication Data

Rowatt, G. Wade.
    Pastoral care with adolescents in crisis.

    Bibliography: p.
    1. Teenagers—Pastoral counseling of. 2. Church work with teenagers. I. Title.
BV4447.R69 1989   259'.23   88-28059
ISBN 0-664-25039-4 (pbk.)

Dedicated to our three children

Wade Clinton Rowatt

John Brock Rowatt

Ashley Jo Rowatt

Contents

Acknowledgments   9

Introduction   11

  1 Adolescents in Crisis   17

  2 Developmental Issues and Crises   29

  3 Principles of Caring   46

  4 Methods for Pastoral Care and Counseling   59

  5 Family Problems   76

  6 Sexual Problems   91

  7 Peer and Academic Pressures   106

  8 Depression and Suicide   119

  9 Substance Abuse   131

10 The Churches Respond   144

Notes   159

Bibliography   165

Acknowledgments

Many persons have contributed in a professional and personal way to the development of this book. By granting and funding my sabbatical leave for a year of focused research, the trustees of The Southern Baptist Theological Seminary, along with President Roy L. Honeycutt and Dean G. Willis Bennett, ensured its completion. From the probing questions and careful dialogue of my teaching colleagues, Clarence Barton, Jan Cox-Gedmark, Bob Cunningham, Michael Hester, Walter Jackson, Andrew Lester, Wayne E. Oates, James Pollard, Edward Thornton, and Ernest White, this book received numerous ideas, redirections, and revisions.

A research grant from the Eli Lilly Foundation through the Union Theological Seminary in Richmond Youth Project funded portions of the social research for this volume. Sara Little and Dan Aleshire offered encouragement along with their support.

G. Randolph Schrodt, M.D., and Barbara A. Fitzgerald, M.D., co-directors of the Adolescent Treatment Program, Norton Psychiatric Clinic, and professors in the Department of Psychiatry and Behavioral Sciences, University of Louisville School of Medicine, provided a clinical setting and professional critique that deepened my understanding of the multidimensional nature of adolescent crises. The outstanding nursing, educational, and other staff members of Six East at Norton provided wisdom and were models of professional care. Their interest in this book kept me involved over the duration. Their work with teenagers was an inspiration.

Over one hundred ministers discussed the needs of teenagers and shared how they attempt to minister in crises. Gwen Alston-Harbuck, Gwynn Davis, Darrel Gabbard, John Hatcher, Mori Hiratoni, Malcolm Marler, Don McMinn, Richard Ross,

Barbara Rubbins, Bob Tallent, T. Scott Wiggington, and John Willingham are but a few to whom I owe a debt of gratitude.

Six graduate students spent one or more semesters ministering with adolescents in crisis and offered their insights for our supervision and seminar context. Thank you, Vance Davis, Mariam Anne Glover, Val Gonzollas, John Gray, Karen Lovett, and Brian Williams.

The courageous youth of Norton Psychiatric Clinic who permitted me to join in their struggle for wholeness sustained me as I walked alongside them during their hospitalization. The teenagers who came for counseling to St. Matthew's Baptist Church and gave me their poems, letters, and diaries have also been my teachers. All these adolescents touched my heart as we journeyed toward health.

I'm grateful to Penny Marler and Ruby Zecker, who assisted with the statistical research. I appreciate the painstaking typing and technical help from Tish Gardiner, Lisa Hutchens, Eileen Long, Jackie Morcom, Fearn Pate, Lisa Redden, and Pam Stallard.

Thanks to Cynthia Thompson, of Westminster / John Knox Press, who provided words of affirmation and appropriate confrontation as this project began. I'm also thankful to Harold Twiss, who took over in mid-course and provided helpful editorial suggestions for the final production.

As always my wife, Jodi, gave loving support and a professional exchange of ideas. Wade C. and J. Brock, my adolescent sons, challenged and enlightened the concepts in this volume. Ashley, my seven-year-old daughter, brought moments of joy to punctuate the laborious task of writing. I thank God again for my family.

Introduction

The purpose of this book is to provide religious workers with principles and methods of caring with young people in crisis. Pastors in local congregations can find insights for their youth programs, ideas for sermon topics, and resources for pastoral care and counseling with teens. Youth ministers (staff and lay volunteers) can deepen their understanding of adolescents and discover ways to participate on the healing team that responds to teenagers in crisis. Chaplains and pastoral counselors can expand their awareness of principles and methods of assessment and counseling with the adolescent population. Students in training for the ministry (who frequently finance their education by part-time youth work in churches) can be introduced to deeper levels of crisis ministry that may otherwise go unnoticed in the youth program. Parents of teens can better understand the context of care for their troubled offspring.

A variety of research avenues and methods have yielded insights, concerns, and data that blend together in the pages that follow. A literature search revealed exciting new reading in fields that exist in near isolation from one another. Legal, medical, educational, and religious research reflected limited cooperation in addressing the problem of adolescents in crisis. Social research on young people provided intriguing summaries that suggest many teens are at risk of major crises.

Interviews with teenagers (aged twelve to nineteen) yielded rich, personal, but often painful stories. The needs of Hispanics, blacks, whites, Asians, and those of mixed race surfaced as sometimes different but more often similar. Social-class differences, not racial ones, loomed large. Young people in religious activities reflected divergent values and attitudes. Urban and rural teens told of varied pressures. Interviews with those

Figure 1. Levels of need for pastoral care with adolescents.

	Ranked by Greatest Need	% None	% Low	% Moderate	% High	% Urgent	% N/A
Depression	7	1	18	40	30	11	
Vocation	6	0	12	41	37	6	4
Self-identity	1	0	2	20	64	14	
Friendships	2	1	3	29	60	11	
Hospitalization	10	5	52	28	5	4	6
Sexual problems	5	1	17	35	33	14	
Alcohol and drugs	4	1	12	32	37	18	
Suicide	9	2	38	26	10	15	1
Parent conflicts	3	0	7	33	43	17	
Religious questions	8	0	10	53	30	6	1
Other		0	1	4	2	2	1

who work with adolescents—psychiatrists, social workers, pastoral counselors, family therapists, attorneys, ministers, group-home staff, public- and private-school teachers, parents, and police—underscored the complexity of the issues facing our youth and demonstrated how training and orientation condition both the definition of the cause of their crises and the preferred treatments, responses, and solutions.

Returns from a brief questionnaire that went to 250 ministers chosen at random from all fifty states validated the breadth of concerns and pointed to unique programs that are evolving in particular churches. The selection was made from the Association for Clinical Pastoral Education and the American Association of Pastoral Counselor Supervisors. Because of my acquaintance with some of these persons, 47 of these questionnaires were returned from Southern Baptist churches. However, 46 came from other churches.

After providing basic demographic data on the size, location, denomination, and number of young people in their congregations, the respondents were asked to check a list of ministries provided to youth. These included such items as home visits, social activities, youth worship, youth education, retreats, hospital visitation, counseling, and legal support. Other ministries provided by their churches could be added. Next, the respondents were asked to evaluate the level of need for pastoral care (see Figure 1) and the effectiveness of the ministry provided (see Figure 2) in a variety of adolescent crises: depression, vocation, self-identity, friendships, hospitalization, sexual problems, alcohol and drugs, suicide, parent conflicts, and religious questions. A space to list other needs was provided.

The ministers were asked to describe effective pastoral care programs provided by their church, to suggest helpful resources for teens, and to name other churches that had creative youth programs.

While there were a few differences (discussed in chapter 10) in the types of problems faced in small churches as opposed to larger congregations, there were not corresponding differences by location and denomination. The level of need for pastoral care to teens varied greatly according to the problems addressed. Most frequently reported as "high" or "urgent" was the need for assistance with identity formation. Next came developing friendships in a peer group. Conflicts with parents was third. Alcohol and drug problems were fourth, and sexual problems fifth. Vocation and depression

Figure 2. Pastoral care programs for adolescent needs.

	Ranked by Effect-iveness	% Not at All	% Poorly	% Moderately	% Good	% Excellent	% N/A
Depression	9	5	20	46	25	0	4
Vocation	10	2	25	42	21	2	7
Self-identity	8	0	10	35	47	4	4
Friendships	2	1	5	37	43	10	4
Hospitalization	4	3	10	28	32	8	9
Sexual problems	7.5	4	23	41	23	3	6
Alcohol and drugs	7.5	3	25	42	23	3	4
Suicide	6	12	17	37	22	7	5
Parent conflicts	5	3	12	47	28	7	4
Religious questions	1	1	6	28	47	13	4
Other				2	1		

were ranked close behind in sixth and seventh places, respectively. Religious questions and suicide claimed moderate attention, but very few persons saw the need for hospital visitation as especially widespread.

This book attempts to summarize reflections from a wide range of sources, to provide understanding for the comprehensive picture of youth crises, and to offer theological illuminations that inform the process of care and counseling with adolescents in crisis. While many readers will no doubt be familiar with the adolescent psychosocial developmental issues described in chapter 1, chapter 2 integrates theological insights, developmental uniquenesses, and the effects of current social pressures. Chapter 3 discusses foundational principles of pastoral care and counseling with teens, and chapter 4 suggests methods for pastoral care. The implementation of the principles and methods unfolds in a variety of common problems: family crises (chapter 5), sexual problems (chapter 6), school and peer problems (chapter 7), depression and suicide (chapter 8), and substance abuse (chapter 9). A concluding chapter summarizes my research findings about expanded, integrated, church-based programs that may actually reduce the level of stress and discusses selected approaches that have in some locations provided successful help for suffering teens.

1

Adolescents in Crisis

Adolescence, the tough, tumultuous, turbulent transition between childhood and adulthood, holds a fascination for children and adults but also generates no small amount of anxiety for both. The teen generation's romanticized image in the mass media induces school-age children to dream of a magic future with love, leisure, and lusty luxury. Elementary-school girls no longer only dress up like Mom; they copy the "jean age" look with designer clothes and their own nail polish. Their male counterparts emulate rock stars, sports idols, and military heroes. While children daydream of that magic thirteenth birthday, many adults frantically attempt to preserve their own vanishing youthful image and dread each passing year. Franchised health clubs entice men and women alike. Aloe-based cosmetics and new miracle chemicals promise "no wrinkles." The right diet supports a prolonged, youthful body. Western adults, like their preteen children, are lured by the adolescent image.

Nevertheless, adolescence also stimulates fears and generates anxieties. Fifth- and sixth-graders frequently dread leaving elementary school and graduating to new pressures. While the level of academic expectations frightens a few, more resistance stems from alarming reports of drugs, violence, sex, and peer rejection. Panic attacks are not uncommon among early adolescents unprepared for the stress of the teen world. One intimidated girl voiced it this way: "I don't want to grow up. I like being protected by Dad and Mother. I'm afraid of what will happen to me."

In reality many teens find their own experiences frustrating and disappointing. The Hollywood portrayal of a teenage fantasyland eludes them, and they experience depression, isolation, confusion, rejection, anger, and loneliness. They feel betrayed when their dreams turn into nightmares. A romantic evening turns into a pregnancy; a dream car wrecks and someone special dies; the substance-induced high crashes; their parents disappoint them; school turns sour.

While adults long for personal youthful experiences, many frequently resist dealing with teens and despairingly decry the day their own offspring will become adolescents. "In this day and age a parent can be thankful just to get them through alive and in one piece," said the father of two high school girls. Not only do parents struggle with teens in their homes, many helping adults avoid teens if they can. Teachers, social workers, physicians, attorneys, and ministers often disdain youth work. One has only to look at the burn-out rate for youth workers to be convinced. It takes a special person to love working with adolescents over the years.

Children and adults may view adolescence with strong ambivalence and attempt to avoid contact, but teens have little choice in the matter. They must face the stressful, changing, and confusing youth culture. It is theirs!

Concerns of Today's Youth

With each new level of solutions (mechanical, electrical, atomic) comes a higher, more complex level of problems. The teens of the 1990s and of the twenty-first century face a complex web of social problems and personal options.

Contemporary Western society offers decreased support while at the same time it contributes to the increased stress level placed on the adolescent generation. More young people grow up in one-parent families. Those who do have both parents in the home spend less time there, and almost all teens are isolated from their extended family of grandparents, aunts, uncles, and cousins. They are less likely to be friends with a caring adult teacher, minister, or coach. The network of supportive, caring people with whom they can interact diminishes or deteriorates and in some cases disappears. Not only does this decrease relationships, it means significantly less support in times of adolescent crisis. A resulting loneliness creates anxiety for teens, and that in turn fuels more "acting out" and "withdrawing" behavior.

However, the major additions to the stress level in the lives of adolescents are the social problems in their world. Their parents may have demonstrated in the streets for social justice in the sixties, but today's youngsters have no forum. Make no mistake; they search desperately to be heard. "Where do we cry 'help'?" asked a sensitive fifteen-year-old girl in Miami, Florida. She went on to say, "I'm afraid of so many things: AIDS, being kidnapped, and terrorist attacks, not to mention that we will all be nuked by someone pushing the wrong button."

Some feel the pressure of being number one. A pastor from Ohio summarized their plight this way: "Stress seems to come from peer and parental pressure to achieve great heights, especially in sports and academics." As Charles Whited reflected in *The Miami Herald,* "Today's world is tough on both parents and kids. At one extreme, the nation's prisons overflow with the offspring of parents who failed. At the other extreme among upward-striving yuppies, you find a fierce drive to create superkids, geared to win honors, be rich, run things."[1]

The concerns expressed by the young people I interviewed reflect new social worries as well as typical adolescent struggles. Dating and sexuality still top the most-often-mentioned list. Problems relating to parents are second; struggling for independence, testing the limits, and checking out the sincerity of love bonds still contribute to a wide generation gap Other typical concerns are body image, vocational decisions, athletic competition, spending money, curfews, telephone time, friends who are unacceptable to their parents, problems in school or in church, getting a car or a driver's license and on and on.

A new group of social concerns includes fears of being abducted, AIDS, depletion of oil resources, homosexual and heterosexual rape, abandonment by parents through divorce or desertion, pollution of the environment, and growing up to find a bureaucratic society that has no place for them "I'm afraid that I'll either never grow up or that, when I do, the world will be so messed up I can't lead a normal life," complained a fifteen-year-old boy in Miami. Two teenage joggers passed me on the beach, wearing matching T-shirts that summed up the contemporary anxiety level. They read, *Save Our Planet.*

Economic shifts and waves of third-world refugees are creating a larger group of poverty-stricken families. Teenage girls who become mothers seldom escape the poverty cycle Young people in poverty families are angry and frustrated to be doing without in the "land of opportunity." The middle class of America is shrinking as the rich get richer and the poor get poorer. Wealthy teens seem to be wandering in meaningless fashion as they search for happiness in European clothes, fast cars, recreational sex, substance abuse, and world travel.

Perhaps as many as 30 to 50 percent of the current teen population will experience a major crisis before reaching the age of eighteen. They will be hospitalized, appear in court, have major parental conflicts, attempt suicide, abuse alcohol or drugs, drop out of school, get pregnant, pay for or have an abortion, or something else of this magnitude. Many will experience multiple crises!

Special pressures abound. Some poverty-stricken teenage females are said to have children for the sake of additional welfare support; some young Asian Americans report excessive family pressure to excel academically. Sons and daughters with athletic, dramatic, or musical talent are pushed to excel in ways that harm their psychosocial development. As the social pressures on young people mount and the support network diminishes, the anxiety level increases. As the anxiety level increases, the number of adolescents in crisis begins to soar.

Other social institutions are attempting to support or replace the family in responding to young people in trouble. These trends reflect the need for more solid, sustaining networks as well as increased levels of crisis counseling. High schools, for instance, are beginning to offer child-care services for teenage mothers. Some large cities have separate schools (grades six to twelve) for teen mothers. Psychiatric treatment centers for adolescents are multiplying around the nation; the federal government has a missing-and-exploited-children's agency. Substance-abuse programs for teens are increasing, although there are long waiting lists. Churches and denominational agencies are responding with special studies and new programs.[2]

Theological Foundations

Caring and counseling, from a religious viewpoint, can best be understood through the image of shepherding. Shepherding is the basic undergirding model for pastoral care and religious counseling. (See Seward Hiltner, *Preface to Pastoral Theology*.) To theoretical foundations drawn from sociology and psychology, shepherding as a theological perspective provides added understanding. This theological dimension primarily distinguishes pastoral care and counseling from other forms of psychotherapy. Trained ministers can be effective psychologists, social workers, and general therapists; when their biblical-theological foundations inform their therapeutic interventions, the care, counseling, or psychotherapy they offer is *pastoral.*

Pastoral care can be defined as a continuing relationship of support and/or confrontation between a minister and an individual or a group in times of developmental or emergency crisis (see Wayne E. Oates, *New Dimensions in Pastoral Care*[3]). Pastoral care is most importantly a relationship. The relationship may be informal, such as casual hallway conversations or across-the-table discussions in a youth lounge, or it may be more formal, "in the office" counseling. In pastoral counseling a specific time, place, and agenda are planned around a therapeutic conversation. In both the formal and informal context the primary key is the relationship. And the relationship is characterized by the shepherding dimension, which will be discussed in more detail in subsequent pages. Pastoral care is with persons, not structural institutions. While social intervention may be a dynamic part of the minister's role, that is outside the scope of care and counseling as defined here. Pastoral care can be with individuals, notably the adolescent in crisis, or with families or groups of adolescents, or with groups of persons important to the adolescent. Pastoral care is not limited to emergencies such as divorce or accident but can also be rendered in developmental crises that emerge as a natural part of the growing process. The birth of a new child may constitute a crisis for the adolescent in that family. Turning sixteen is another developmental crisis.

While professional pastoral care and counseling organizations are twentieth-century phenomena and while research from the behavioral sciences informs modern pastoral care practices, the shepherding stance toward persons in crisis is an ancient biblical concept. Perhaps the shepherding principles are most clearly articulated in Psalm 23 and in Matthew's Gospel (25:40), where Jesus promises that "as you did it to one of the least of these my brethren, you did it to me," as he speaks of the poor, the naked, the sick, the imprisoned, and the hungry. Pastoral care and counseling appear throughout the scriptures as the shepherding of suffering persons.

Historically, shepherding as a pastoral care perspective developed as a theological dimension in the works of Seward Hiltner, but it has been addressed by many others. An approach that integrates the shepherding perspective of Hiltner with later developments in pastoral care and counseling suggests six interrelated primary dimensions of the shepherding task. These six dimensions—healing, reconciling, sustaining, confronting, guiding, and informing—are woven together in the care and counseling approach to crisis. For the sake of clarity, these dimensions will be analyzed separately; however, in practice one can hardly label a particular ministry response to a crisis as *only* sustaining or *only* confronting or *only* guiding. One of these dimensions may dominate, but the others remain. Caring ministry as a response to crisis reflects some of all six dimensions. The shepherding approach assists persons to face crisis and to experience the richness and fullness of a holistic relationship to themselves, to their environment, and to the future because of the hope they find in God.

Dimensions of Shepherding

A brief definition of the six dimensions of shepherding is necessary for a discussion of their interrelatedness.

Healing is a process of assisting persons to move toward wholeness, especially in the light of the brokenness brought about by crisis.

Reconciling is a process of assisting persons to move toward restoring wholeness in broken or strained relationships with those who constitute their social environment.

Sustaining is a process of supporting persons by standing by them and bearing burdens with them while responding to the crisis.

Confronting is a process of moving against the thoughts, feelings, assumptions, or behavioral patterns of persons in response to the crisis.

Guiding is a process of assisting persons to make decisions by drawing from within them what was potentially available in their own decision-making.

Informing is a process of clarifying alternatives for persons by providing specific new information and data.

Reconciling and Healing

The foundational question in a shepherding response to crisis involves a polarity between reconciling and healing. What is the goal? The crisis caregiver or counselor holds healing and reconciliation in dynamic tension and responds by suggesting the possibility of both. While healing is the ultimate goal for the individual in crisis, reconciling is the primary objective for the individual's relationships to others in the crisis. Both find significance as shepherding ministry from the biblical perspective.

The four Gospels record twenty-six cases, excluding the parallels, of individuals who were healed by Jesus. The language of salvation itself blends with the language of healing throughout the New Testament. Jesus frequently intertwined the dimensions of physical healing and personal wholeness or salvation in his ministry. For instance, as he healed the man sick of palsy who was lowered through the roof in the midst of the crowd (Mark 2:1–2), Jesus performed the healing miracle there as a prerequisite for the faith necessary for wholeness *and* salvation. Also in the epistles, Paul's work in healing supports the view of the early Christians that physical and spiritual wholeness are interwoven.

Ministers concerned with healing and reconciliation with adolescents in crisis are cautioned to avoid two common errors. On the one hand, they might inappropriately push the question of the adolescent's relationship to God in a way that angers the adolescent enough to break the counseling relationship and terminate further caregiving. However, on the other hand, they need to avoid the assumption that no examination of faith is appropriate. A crisis will raise questions of one's faith stance (particularly in reflecting). Ultimate questions for reflection come after the crisis has passed its critical point and will focus around one's relationships, around one's view of self, and around the future. These each have a theological dimension. Relationship to the self begins with a belief in the goodness (or the evil) of creation and continues with understanding the meaning of redemption and incarnation. The relationship to self is ultimately asked: "Am I a person of worth, created in the image of God, loved by God, and therefore of value?" Questions about relationships are basically faith queries. "Can one's environment be trusted? Are the powers of light able to sustain the battle against the powers of darkness?" The response of persons of faith is that "the light shines in the darkness, and the darkness has not overcome it" (John 1:5). Facing one's environment is ultimately a question of faith. Facing the future is fundamentally a theological question of hope. The foundation of hope from a religious perspective is in the working of a Being greater than all personhood, but it is not devoid of the responsibility of persons and the goodness of persons.

While ministers are cautioned against prematurely and inappropriately pushing religious questions into a crisis situation, they must also be cautioned not to ignore the impact of faith questions on the response to the crisis.

Healing of the person is a primary goal, but healing cannot be understood apart from reconciliation with one's environment. No person can be whole and remain isolated from meaningful relatedness. Crises can result from broken relationships, but more frequently they *produce* broken relationships.

Reconciliation, a major theme of Christian scripture, is a process of restoring broken or strained relationships between persons, individuals, and God. Reconciliation is bridge-building over the troubled waters of crisis. Reconciliation is the caring minister's response to disunity and brokenness. The incarnation has at its heart reconciling persons to God. Paul appeals for reconciliations many times but most notably in the dispute over the differentness of spiritual gifts (1 Cor. 12:21–26). Shepherding as a ministry of reconciliation attempts to assist adolescents to see their place in the family, with their peers, and in society at large and to equip them to live in growing, mutually enhancing relationships.

Reconciliation, built upon several theological themes, involves awareness of the brokenness, confession of one's own participation in the brokenness, however large or small that might seem, and the giving and receiving of forgiveness. Sometimes a ritual of acceptance such as the verbal pronouncement of a blessing on the adolescent serves as a powerful symbol of reconciliation in times of crisis. However, most often a hug, a handshake, a gift, or a shared moment of laughter becomes the unlabeled ritual of reconciliation.

Confronting and Sustaining

Healing the self and reconciling with the environment remain in tension as the shepherd responds to a crisis. Two relationship stances can be taken toward both healing and reconciliation. They are confronting and sustaining. These two stances must also be held in dynamic tension.

Like healing and reconciling, confronting and sustaining are biblical models for a shepherding ministry. Confronting is the application of the law, while sustaining is more an expression of grace. Confronting occurs throughout the scriptures and can mean moving against the environment as well as against a person's assumptions, thoughts, feelings, or behavioral patterns. The prophets spoke boldly, not only to individuals, as in the confrontation of King David for his involvement with Bathsheba, but also to environments, as the prophets Jeremiah and Amos spoke to the culture of their time.

Furthermore, in Matthew's Gospel, Jesus provides a model for confronting. In Matthew 18:15–22, the disciples are instructed to confront a "brother" if they feel wronged by him. Jesus' model of individual, personal confrontation sets the goal of dealing with one's self confessionally and being restored to wholeness with one's environment. If the confrontation cannot be handled individually in dealing with the self, others are involved until the confrontation is resolved or the individual is excluded from the group. With adolescents and broken family relationships, there is a time when out-of-home placements and changing environments is the ultimate theological response.

Jesus confronted not only individuals but also the culture of his time, seeking reconciliation between individuals and their environment. You can see as Jesus speaks to oppressed and persecuted persons (such as the woman taken in adultery) that he seeks reconciliation in the environment. Paul, reflecting upon this ministry, writes in Galatians 3:28 that in Christ there is no male or female, no Jew or Greek, no bond or free. Confrontation has its ultimate goal—total reconciliation and healing.

Ministers must be careful to note that the authority of confrontation does not come from one's own personality and perceived superior ability but from one's role as a representative of the congregation, the society, and the word of God. The authority and privilege of confrontation are expressed as a representative of something larger than one's self. We must take care not to risk rejecting individuals through unrealistic private confrontations. Ultimately, the confrontation should be such that persons feel they have encountered a truth larger than themselves and the individual with whom they speak. The truth of confrontation produces hope when shared in the context of love.

Sustaining exists in dynamic tension with confrontation as the fourth shepherding dimension. Sustaining, like confrontation, is an approach of bringing wholeness to a self and reconciliation to the environment. Sustaining consists of supporting persons by standing by them in their quest for healing and reconciliation. Understanding, feeling with, and accepting an individual moves them toward wholeness and is at the heart of the sustaining process.

The sustaining aspect of shepherding is also seen throughout the Old and New Testaments. God is with the bewildered and lost slaves in Egypt and sustains them in their pilgrimage through the wilderness as they move toward their future in the promised land. Galatians 6:2 admonishes Christians to "bear one another's burdens." Sustaining, a continuing process of seeking to preserve hope, encourages self-acceptance. In the face of a crisis, adolescents sometimes overgeneralize and magnify problems out of proportion. Sustaining teens as individuals maintains a degree of self-respect and hope.

In a time of crisis, sustaining the environment may also be needed. The adolescent's parents, siblings, extended family, peers, and perhaps teachers and others all need a word of encouragement from the caregiver. The caregiver can be an advocate for the adolescent, thus sustaining efforts toward reconciliation in the present or at some point in the future.

Confronting and sustaining are maintained in tension without either excluding the other from the context of caregiving. Wayne Oates uses the analogy of hand surgery in discussing his approach to shepherding. Early hand surgeons would literally hold the hand of the patient in one hand while performing the surgery with their other hand. The underneath hand symbolizes the sustaining, while the hand with the surgical instrument represents the confrontation. Both are necessary.

In a team approach to adolescent ministry, it is not unusual for some members to take a confrontive, hard-line, maintain-the-rules, administrative approach to a given adolescent in crisis, while other members of the team take a supportive, understanding, "I'm-your-friend" approach. These representations of law and grace are easier to make when a team is responding to the crisis, but sometimes both must be made by one person. A single caregiver can maintain the tension between confronting and sustaining as the process of responding to the crisis unfolds.

Guiding and Informing

A third set of shepherding polarities, guiding and informing, are similarly to be held in tension. Both guiding and informing are perspectives for confronting and sustaining, which are in turn perspectives for healing and reconciling. An attempt to provide new information produces the confrontation. At other times, guiding the person's thoughts and reflections leads to self-confrontation. Likewise, in sustaining individuals and environments, informing will be the approach at times. In other situations, guiding individuals to examine their own thoughts and reflections will lead to sustaining.

Like confronting, sustaining, reconciling, and healing, guiding has its foundation in Christian scripture. Guiding is seen throughout the Old Testament, where both the prophets and the priests proclaim and teach the word of God in hope of a response from their listeners. Furthermore, as Jesus talks with the accusers about to stone the woman taken in adultery, he draws out of them the criteria for making their decision. In John 8:7 he demands, "Let him who is without sin among you be the first to throw a stone." As the hearers reflect on the implications of his statement, they turn one at a time to leave. They have been guided in the process of making their own decision, never directly informed of the decision Jesus would have made.

Guiding (this process of helping persons discover within themselves the resources for making decisions) involves reflection upon thoughts, feelings, attitudes, and behaviors. Adolescents in particular may need assistance in differentiating between their thoughts, feelings, and attitudes. *Feeling Good* by David Burns provides excellent information in the process of examining and differentiating thoughts, feelings, and attitudes.[4] Guiding is an integral part of shepherding ministry when choices are offered by the person in crisis and examined in light of their understanding of potential outcomes. In direct contrast to guiding, informing brings information from outside the individual to bear upon confrontation and sustaining.

Informing, a process of clarifying alternatives by providing specific new information, also has a broad foundation in Christian scripture. In Isaiah 40:28–31 the prophet questions his listeners: "Have you not known? Have you not heard? The Lord is the everlasting God. He does not faint or grow weary. . . . Even youths shall faint and be weary . . . ; but they who wait for the Lord shall renew their strength, they shall mount up with wings like eagles, they shall run and not be weary, they shall walk and not faint." This information is provided as a form of sustaining individuals and their environment in a time of crisis.

In the New Testament we see an example of informing as a means of sustaining individuals and confronting their time of grief when Paul, writing to the church at Thessalonica (I Thess. 4:16), addresses their concern for Christians who have died before Christ's return. Their grief over the loss of their fellow Christians is both confronted and sustained by Paul as he writes, "The dead in Christ will rise first." The shepherding response of informing involves input of new data.

Informing has long been a part of Christian ministry, but it has not regularly been incorporated in shepherding. The teaching and preaching ministries of the church have highlighted the imparting of new information. However, shepherding, caregiving, and counseling can also be avenues of providing new information. Perhaps in the way questions are asked, information voids can be revealed and appropriate responses made. For example, a young man in a substance-abuse crisis can be asked about the substance's effects and then information provided if he does not have accurate data. Informing may take the part of educating adolescents as to the consequences of their behavior or pointing them toward information from other resources that can be applied in a particular crisis.

In summary, shepherding ministry has as its primary goal bringing wholeness to individuals and reconciliation to their environment in a context of hope. Frequently, confronting and sustaining are relationship stances between the counselor, the individual, and the environment. Informing and guiding are perspectives for confronting and sustaining and likewise are to be held in dynamic tension.[5]

2

Developmental Issues and Crises

The concept of adolescence as a long transition between childhood and adulthood does not appear in the biblical text. Children receive focused attention; however, after puberty they are addressed as young men and women. Adolescence as a psychosocial moratorium between childhood and adulthood appears to be a relatively recent concept arising from the increased occupational demands for more advanced skills during the rise of capitalism and the industrial revolution.[1] A lack of well-defined periods of adolescence in some undeveloped and primitive societies calls into question the assumption that the social aspects of adolescents observed in modern Western society are tied primarily to biological changes. Teens have adult bodies, but they have no adult role. As David Elkind proclaims, they are all grown up with no place to go.[2]

The period of adolescence begins earlier and lasts longer for many of today's young people. Ten-, eleven-, and twelve-year-olds who have not reached puberty are rushed into dating, attending parties, and social functions that were once reserved for teenagers. This creates a stage of preadolescence, when children aren't permitted to be children but are pushed into teen activities. At the other end of adolescence, many adults in their early twenties remain dependent on their parents and have trouble leaving the protection of home. My research focuses primarily on thirteen- to nineteen-year-olds, but professionals responding to young people in crisis need to be aware that role and relationships, not age, define adolescence.

While adolescence represents a term of delayed adulthood, it also provides an opportunity for growth and development. The foundation stones of personhood are set during childhood, but adolescence represents a second chance for mature development.[3] This second chance comes at a time of major cognitive advancements and greatly increased verbal skills. Readers will be familiar with the teen developmental process (having experienced it), so only a brief review is provided here, along with considerations for each stage's impact on crisis needs. Physical, emotional, intellectual, social, and spiritual dynamics interrelate in unique patterns during early, middle, and late adolescence.

Early Adolescence

Early adolescence, usually the period of twelve through fourteen years of age, may begin slightly earlier for girls and later for boys. It is a time of rapid change and adjustment.

Changes

Early adolescence, introduced formally by the onset of puberty, demands adjustment to a multitude of resulting **physical changes**. Both girls and boys are likely to experience uneven spurts of growth. Their sexual organs mature and body hair begins to appear. These changes are likely to produce a sense of awkwardness and inability to control body movements gracefully. Boys sometimes have difficulty accepting their new body image, and girls may react with either shyness or pride. It is not uncommon for both boys and girls to experience an increase in appetite, perhaps resulting in chubbiness for those who do not get enough exercise.

Since girls may develop somewhat more quickly, they are likely to be taller than boys of the same age. This can create some envy on the part of the boys and confusion in the relationships between boys and girls. Chemical changes in the body are likely to lead to acne or other skin problems, which adds to concerns about acceptance by the peer group. Attention to cleanliness and body odor will need to be increased. Social acceptance relates to body image. Tall, muscular boys and thin girls are more highly valued and rewarded in Western society.

These physical developments precipitate a multitude of **emotional changes**. Basically, early adolescents react to chemical and physical changes by being on an emotional roller coaster. They go from despondence and vegetation to excitement and activity for no apparent reason. Although as their body adjusts to chemical changes, some fluctuation of emotion is expected, emotional change is more often tied to confusion around their new role. Their relationship with their parents is shifting, their relationship to their own body is changing, and their relationship with their peers undergoes a transformation. All this can lead to self-doubt, negative thoughts, and depression.

Depression in early adolescents is difficult to assess because of their natural mood swings. Early adolescents may find warmth and intimacy difficult as they pull back from the opposite-sexed parent and awkwardly befriend the same-sexed parent. Younger juveniles often have difficulty handling angry feelings, which surface because of a multitude of unmet expectations, disappointments, and perceived attacks on their self-image.

While these physical and emotional changes are taking place, a number of **intellectual changes** are also occurring. Early adolescents move out of the concrete stage and into what the noted psychologist Jean Piaget has called "informal operations." Basically, they are beginning to differentiate between opposites and to understand gradations of meaning. They will see not only the positive and negative but many alternatives on a variety of issues. They are capable of understanding principles of substitution and reciprocity as characterized mathematically by the understanding of algebra but socially by the understanding of the complexities of their social and political environment.

As might be expected, these physical, emotional, and intellectual changes interact to bring about a number of **social changes**. The early adolescent's relationship to family, peers, and other adults undergoes alterations. While the early adolescent is still physically dependent on his or her family, a subtle shift toward dependence on peers for emotional reinforcement begins. Family is still the primary determinant of moral values and is responsible for setting limits. However, this is a desirable time for the family to begin shifting the responsibility of setting limits from the parents to the adolescent. The family's values, structures, and rules have been a type of shell around the developing offspring. Limits, like the shell of a lobster, protected the child. Transferring the setting of limits to the young person means removing the shell and developing an internal, moral skeletal system. Parents are encouraged to discuss decisions more openly with young adolescents and to anticipate some input from them about limit setting. For example, curfews will still need to be set by the parents but in dialogue with the young person. Parents will find that at social gatherings their offspring want more independence.

Early adolescent peer relationships also begin to undergo a transformation. While most stay primarily in groups of the same sex, some heterosexual pairing off begins. If this does not receive adequate supervision and guidance, sexual crises can arise when emotions and temptations get out of control. On the other hand, if there is not enough opportunity for hetero-sexual relationships to develop, some adolescents will begin to rebel. Latch-key children with too little supervision are prime candidates for sexual crises, like the fourteen-year-old who told of being made pregnant in her home after school by a nineteen-year-old neighbor.

There is a sense of awkwardness between childhood friends who reach adolescence at different stages. There is often a reshuffling of the peer group, which can result in painful exclusions as well as exciting new acceptances.

Early adolescents need responsible peer groups to begin providing opportunities to develop independence from the parents. These groups need supervision by adults and are likely to be the source of affirmation as well as new ideas. Early adolescents need opportunities to relate to these adults (coaches, teachers, ministers, etc.). Obviously these relation-ships need to be characterized by responsibility on the part of these adults, who reinforce the parents' authority but also pro-vide opportunities for young people to ventilate their pent-up emotions.

There are also changes in the **faith development** of early adolescents as they let go of the borrowed faith of their child-hood, which was primarily comprised of a list of hero stories and rules to be followed, and gain information about new areas of moral choice. Early adolescents need education in a variety of moral values as they move from a rules-keeping ethic to an ethic of justice and love in the areas of substance abuse, rela-tionships, world hunger, ecology, and general interpersonal morality. Early adolescents still find the locus of authority for their belief system in their parents and ministers. However, they will be keenly aware of any inconsistencies in the thinking of these persons and be personally damaged by any lapses of moral behavior that they perceive in the lives of their authority figures. The early adolescent's faith takes on a personalized dimension. Hope becomes a new friend for combating depression. The circle of expression of love is expanded to include persons outside of one's own social circle. However, sin is still primarily seen as breaking the rules or not keeping one's promises.

Needs to Be Assessed in a Crisis

Having considered these developmental issues, let us say by way of summary that early adolescents need a sense of **positive self-identification** in the face of the changes brought on by puberty. They need avenues of success in their social activities and intellectual endeavors. They need the support of both parents as caring adults in finding these moments of success. Well-adjusted early adolescents develop an expanded sense of appreciation for humor and celebration, especially in their religious activities. They need space to celebrate and to let down their hair, so to speak.

Early adolescents are also beset by a multitude of eruptive **developmental crises**, which come from within themselves. For instance, early adolescents would experience anxiety in a crisis from a reshuffling of their peer group. They might consider it a crisis the first time they were aware of the full force of their anger toward their own parent. They might experience it as a crisis if they were ahead or behind their peer group in physical or psychosocial development. They need permission to discuss these changes and find support for the person they are becoming. They need forgiveness for awkward mistakes and new space to grow in the family system. However, some early adolescents have so little family, peer, and other adult support that they are besieged by a number of emergencies.

Obviously, early adolescents would perceive the loss of a parent by death, an accident to themselves requiring hospitalization, the divorce of their parents, or a forced move to a new school or community as a disruptive crisis. In such times, early adolescents especially need information about the crisis, a sustaining environment characterized by hope, and avenues of forgiveness for real or imaginary guilt. In a time of crisis, adolescents need from their parents and those who care for them a supportive relationship that permits the discussion of uncomfortable questions. They need referrals to adequate sources of information. They need permission to speak of previously taboo topics. Also, early adolescents in a time of crisis need concrete information about their future and that of their family. They need some sense of inclusion in discussions about the years ahead and a real sense of being important as decisions are made final.

While they need an opportunity to participate in personal and family decisions, they need the reassurance that their parents are still in charge. Limits signal security. If their parents are not present, youngsters need the reassurance of knowing who *will* be in charge. Perhaps a caregiver in crisis intervention will be the only person who looks out for an early teen's well-being.

Middle Adolescence

Middle adolescence usually encompasses fifteen through seventeen years of age. It is a time of expansion and experimentation. The bridge between early and middle adolescence is sometimes difficult to discern. However, middle adolescents are characterized by more fully transforming physiological changes and movement away from their parents. They venture into new and expanding peer relationships.

Changes

Like early adolescence, middle adolescence often occurs earlier in American girls than in boys. Some researchers suggest a lack of meaningful contact with the father as a contributing factor. In societies where father and mother both participate in child-rearing, boys and girls mature at the same rate. Middle adolescence, a time of experimentation with ideas, feeling, and behaviors, brings an expansion of social relationships.

The **physical characteristics** of middle adolescence involve few abrupt changes, but a general refinement of physiological development consolidates a unique body image. Care for the body in terms of cleanliness, exercise, and diet reflects a new concern for self-image. Generally, as adolescents develop a positive body image, a healthy overall self-image grows. However, dangers exist for those who become obsessed with body type. Obesity is also a common teen crisis and is not easily hidden.

Adolescent females' preoccupation with thinness often leads to bulimia or anorexia (see chapter 9). Their desire to become extremely thin can distort their self-perception and become a compulsive effort to lose too much weight. Girls who do not eat properly can retard their normal body growth. However, they apparently return to their growth rate when proper diet is resumed. Boys may become compulsive about muscle-building and turn to steroids. This can lead to psychological disturbances and uncontrolled aggression. A balanced concern for growth expands interest from weight lifting to exercising and general body conditioning. Traditionally, girls concentrate on aerobic classes, and boys choose jogging and competitive sports with their peers. However, both sexes can now turn to a variety of physical exercises.

Middle teens develop a nearly adult body and face decisions about their new, powerful sexual urges. Peer groups seem to re-form, differentiating those who become sexually active from those who do not. Estimates vary widely, but from 20 to 75 percent of middle adolescents are likely to be sexually active, which sets them at danger for a number of crises, including pregnancy, sexually transmitted diseases (STDs), emotional rejection, abuse, rape, and homosexuality.

Furthermore, middle adolescence is a time of expanding **emotional development** and brings new depths of depression, anger, and anxiety. These are likely to develop alongside the social freedom that comes to middle adolescents. The fluctuating highs and lows of early adolescence commonly stabilize in middle adolescence. However, there is an increased danger of sustained levels of depression. Not only does the intensity of negative emotions increase in middle adolescence, but the range of feelings related to an expanded social involvement and new areas of experimentation are often confusing. "I've never felt this way before" is a frequent complaint of bewildered middle teens. For the first time, they deal with new levels of sexual excitement, temptation, guilt, and perhaps even shame. Those who lack sustained care also develop new levels of fear. The loss of their earlier blind trust and a few bad experiences open their eyes to a multitude of dangers. Frequently in their attempt to avoid negative emotions, adolescents will become chronically busy and form cliques for security. Some turn to the great escapes of alcohol, drugs, and partying. A few might develop hallucinations and fantasies to escape the agony and pain of their emotional conflict and turmoil. While hallucinations might be drug-related or very early psychotic signals, many are conversion reactions; that is, they develop as a block to any activity that produces uncontrolled anxiety. For example, a person who fears the temptation of peeking into windows may become functionally blind. A teen who fears some temptation may become immobilized by hallucinations.

Adolescents in this expanding time tend to think of themselves as the center of their emotional world. They will be most concerned with what brings pleasure to them and will demonstrate only a limited capacity for sacrificing their own pleasure for the pleasure of others or for the benefit of their family or community. Much of the motivation comes from a philosophy of "If it feels good, I want to try it." They attempt to avoid boredom at all costs. But they need more than entertainment; they need a challenge at a deeper emotional level.

Middle-adolescent thought patterns and **intellectual processing** are also in an expansive mode. Middle adolescents are more likely to have moved farther away from concrete thinking into abstractions. They are able to think symbolically and give new meaning to their world and to their faith. Middle adolescents who continue to mature are less impulsive about decisions and can compare their views and conclusions against the responses of others. This new ability to think critically about alternatives and issues can be a positive resource for dealing with crises. A simple process of (1) differentiating problems so that each problem can be defined, (2) generating alternatives, (3) assessing the probable personal impact of each alternative, and (4) deciding on a plan of action aids many adolescents in developmental and emergency crises. Middle adolescents will be able to handle this process and seek less advice from their caregivers than will early adolescents. However, middle adolescents are egocentric; they still think more in terms of the effect of a crisis on themselves than on others, although this is not as pronounced as in childhood and early adolescence. They also think in the present. Because they perceive time as moving slowly (a month is a long time), they fail to evaluate long-range effects of their decisions. Because of their increased capacity for critical and reflective thinking, middle adolescents are likely to challenge inconsistencies and injustices in their family, school, work, peer, and church environment. Although they are not as idealistic as late adolescents, they still tend to think in terms of *what* is right as well as *who* is right. Depressed youth can be naturally expected to focus their perceptions on themselves and to suffer an increase in cognitive distortions.

Middle adolescence is a time of expanded **social activities** and a further weakening of parental ties. As middle adolescents develop new friends, they pull farther away from the family group. They will spend much of their time with the peer group and bring frustration to adults who try to maintain family time together. Parents who themselves are caught up in a hectic pace may be relieved by their children's lack of demands on their time and lured into a false sense of security that their offspring no longer need them. Middle adolescents will have frequent sibling squabbles with younger children at home as they attempt to differentiate themselves from the family structure. Middle adolescents begin to develop relationships with other adult family members or nonfamily mentors. In settings where the extended family still lives in close proximity, aunts, uncles, older cousins, and grandparents may serve as adult friends who assist in beginning the movement away from the nest.

However, because of the rapid mobility of Western society, many young people do not have the luxury of extended family members who live nearby. Therefore, the middle adolescent must turn to the community or the church family to find someone to serve as a role model. This may be a coach, a youth minister, a teacher, or a neighbor. Young people who have no positive mentor are prime targets for pushers and pimps and perhaps gangs. A positive adult relationship is important because the adult serves as a transition object during detachment from the family and attachment to the external world. This transition usually begins in middle adolescence but may never take place. Parents need to bless their middle adolescent's friendship with an appropriate and respected adult. It is a good idea to form relationships at work or church where children can know appropriate adults before reaching the middle adolescent years.

Because of their new ability to think critically and to reflect on inconsistencies, middle adolescents develop an expanded capacity for **faith experience**. They will ask new questions about the scriptures, about their own church's doctrine, about other faiths, and particularly about justice issues. They find themselves blaming God for what seems to be an unfair event or crisis in their lives. They may blame God for letting a parent lose a job or for the death of a friend in a car wreck. Usually they cannot verbalize these feelings toward God without the assistance of a caring counselor. However, they will act out by drawing back from church and becoming less involved in religious activities.

Middle adolescents develop and build new rituals and examine new faith issues. They become interested in new musical experiences. They enjoy expressing faith through the music of their day. Churched middle adolescents may be fond followers of Christian rock groups and Christian rock radio stations.

Needs to Be Assessed in a Crisis

In a time of crisis, middle adolescents have needs to be assessed that differ from those of early adolescence. Middle adolescents, like early adolescents, face both developmental and emergency crises. Their needs vary.

Several common **developmental crises** illustrate these needs. One common adjustment focuses around accepting responsibility for transportation and driving a car. Gaining the necessary knowledge, skills, and attitudes about responsibility for transportation is essential before an adolescent can take part in Western society. Dating is also a typical middle-adolescent developmental adjustment that brings its special needs. Obviously, there is a need for understanding oneself sexually as male or female and for developing an informed, safe, and responsible attitude about one's sexuality. Dating brings new levels of intense joy, excitement, and affirmation, but it also provides an equal potential for new depths of grief, rejection, and pain. A lost boyfriend or girlfriend frequently causes adolescent thoughts of suicide, for example (see chapter 8).

Distance from parents, a third developmental issue for middle adolescents, is understood in terms of freedom. Middle adolescents typically express this need in such statements as "Why can't my parents understand that I can think for myself and make decisions by myself? My parents need to know that I have a mind of my own; I'm not a baby any more." Parents who are too strict urge their strong children toward rebellion, while they nudge offspring of lesser ego strength into a premature foreclosure on their identity. However, parents who provide few stable values in limit-setting leave children in danger of creating crises by experimenting beyond their capacity for self-control. Adolescents with great ego strength will be able to set limits for themselves, but those with weaker ego strength may fall off either end of a continuum. Some will become so anxious and frightened by freedom that they begin to deteriorate emotionally, while others will become so enamored of freedom that they act out behaviorally.

In addition to developmental crises, middle adolescents

have unique needs in time of **emergency crisis**. The major emergencies for them are related to substance abuse, sex, depression, academics, and, of course, the family. If the family system deteriorates, middle adolescents will frequently blame themselves and grieve deeply. Grief over the end of their parents' marriage and unbearable self-blame, for example, may lead to acting out sexually, to attempting to escape into alcohol and drug abuse, or to hedonistic pleasure-seeking. Addicted adolescents may need out-of-home placement or a substitute family while they are repairing the relationships with their own families. Those with substance abuse problems, including food and eating disorders, need a program not only to assist them in getting off drugs, perhaps a residential treatment program, but also to assist them in learning to manage the negative thoughts and feelings that have led to such behavior.

Middle adolescents more frequently become behavior problems in school or in the neighborhood. They need firm but loving control and discipline by persons who have previously established a caring relationship. They benefit from programs of value clarifications that stress internalizing the value system. They usually are not motivated by fear of external reprisals.

Middle adolescents may have sexual crises such as the fathering or conceiving of a child out of wedlock. A few ox pressed fears of being sexually abused by an adult (and not always outside the family). While adolescents need room to find their own sexual values, they need enough education and guidance not to abuse or be abused sexually.

In this time of expansion and exploration, middle adolescents need time and space to reflect and learn from their emergency crises. They need some system of forgiveness for their own mistakes and also an experience of grace that accepts their attempts to discover themselves. While they must admit their mistakes, they need reassurance that they did not cause all their problems.

However, experimentation is more likely in middle adolescence to lead to accidents and illness. Young people need good medical care, but, even more, they need the space to talk about major concerns during this care. Their worries are more likely to be developmental than physical and death-related. For example, a fifteen-year-old boy, hospitalized for tests for meningitis, did not share his parents' anxiety about his health but was very concerned about what the hospitalization would mean for his chances to make the high school football team that fall. Teens need the opportunity and space to talk about the impact of an illness on the rest of their lives.

Spiritually, middle adolescents need an opportunity to learn about their own faith system from a depth perspective and to make decisions about the faith systems of their peers. They need an opportunity to ask questions about other religious groups, including unusual sects. Usually these questions indicate that they are looking for authority in an idealized value system in the face of disillusionment in their own family and faith.

Late Adolescence

Late adolescence is not so much a matter of chronology as it is a shift from experimentation to a mode of refinement and consolidation. While almost all early adolescents move into the experimentation issues of middle adolescence, not all middle adolescents mature enough to struggle with late adolescence issues. Some stagnate in the experimental stage of middle adolescence.

Changes

Although some young people never stop experimenting, one would normally expect eighteen- or nineteen-year-olds to move into adultlike processes of refinement and consolidation. It is time to refine the data gathered through their experimentation and to consolidate those data into a view of self, society, sacredness, and the future. For persons not able to move into late adolescence, the experimentation stage may continue into the twenties and beyond. Adult daredevils still abound. Perhaps these persons need at some point a moratorium from responsibility of life, where they can back up and work through refinement and consolidation issues again. For some persons, experimentation in delayed adolescence becomes a lifestyle, uncritically adopted, until a mid-life crisis forces the refinement and consolidation task upon them.

Physical changes occur as the late adolescent's body is consolidated into an adult image. Late adolescence is usually the end of the period of growth and body development and is the time for lifelong decisions to be made about diet and exercise. It is the time for developing attitudes and values about one's sexuality. Young people need to learn to care for themselves in independent living arrangements. This involves not only money but the basic necessities of cleaning, cooking, and running a household. It seems apparent today that both men and women are expected to maintain themselves in independent living. The impact of the feminist movement seems greatest in young women's expectations, as they prepare themselves not so much to care for a man as to live their own lives. However, many late-adolescent males have not adopted complementary views; they still expect to find a woman to take care of them. Many are rudely awakened, and many young marriages experience difficulty as conflicts over expectations arise.

Settling into an **emotional style** begins with discovering how one's identity impacts one's environment. The emotional volatility of early and middle adolescence levels out. Late adolescents settle into an emotional pattern where they can effectively give and receive affirmation and affection and where they have a conflict management style that permits them to deal with anger in constructive ways. They strive to "be angry but not sin" (see Eph. 4:26). As they learn to deal with aggression, they negotiate new relationships with their peers, parents, and persons of authority. Stabilization of anxiety, fears, and guilt often occurs alongside the anger issue. This is most effectively handled through development of a personalized faith and a reflective stance toward one's belief system that builds respect for persons of varied lifestyles.

Late adolescents, capable of complex and intricate thought patterns, are perhaps in their most creative, imaginative **intellectual phase**. Their abilities, limited not so much by a lack of cognitive development as a lack of knowledge and educational training, vary widely from individual to individual. Their reflective powers and memory permit gifted late adolescents who pursue higher education to challenge even their best professors. Their capacity to think critically about their life and their relationships to others seems almost limitless. However, intelligence, imagination, and a critical reflective process are not to be confused with wisdom, which the late adolescent frequently lacks but will develop through effectively processing life's journey with its mountains and valleys, light and shadow.

For those adolescents who do struggle with refinement and consolidation of **social relationships**, there is a questioning of values and the refining of a personal philosophy of life. This refinement usually brings a final consolidation of the peer groups. When older teens congregate in homogeneous peer groups, these become the basis for lifelong friendships. In the refinement stage, adolescents are more likely to develop friendships that are not necessarily of a dating nature with members of the opposite sex.

Furthermore, the refinement and consolidation process is seen in the area of academic studies and skill development. Vocation, a major decision facing late adolescents, becomes a serious social task. Interests, skills, and knowledge are refined and consolidated toward a given vocation, and peer support and feedback become important. Theological concepts of calling are very important for adolescents embroiled in a vocational struggle.

As late adolescents refine and consolidate their identity, they are able to make covenants and commitments with friends and peers that form lasting relationships. Likewise, as they are able to stabilize their identity, they are capable of making a covenant and commitment to a vocation.

Refinement and consolidation of dating relationships begin during late adolescence. Dating ceases to be primarily a way of learning social skills (early adolescence) and of recreation (middle adolescence), but becomes a way of selecting one's future spouse. Decisions about marriage and vocation are often delayed in favor of continued education. Young women are increasingly choosing to pursue a vocation or career rather than to marry. If marriage does not come toward the end of late adolescence, at least the decision *not* to marry at this time must be resolved.

Late adolescence is also a time of refinement and consolidation of relationships toward parents. Damage to the generation gap can be immense during this phase if parents fail to bless not only the new refined and consolidated identity of their offspring but their move toward independence. When parents support the journey into independence, they lay the foundation for interdependence where they and their adult children build more meaningful friendships.

By late adolescence young people will reject their childhood **faith system** through either rebellion or refinement. Many teens turn from their childhood and early adolescent religiosity toward a pursuit of personal faith. Those who rebel and reject their faith system may prematurely adopt a philosophy of life that excludes faith from the realm of their conscious concerns. Others may seek to replace their childhood faith with the borrowed faith of a new religious leader. While rejecting the authority of their parents' faith, they may blindly accept the authority of a cultic leader or a charismatic religious person. This faith will serve them no better than their childhood faith, but times of crisis, not lectures from their parents, will reveal this. Late adolescents who do reflect upon and refine their childhood faith start on a path of religious enlightenment that can become a lifelong pilgrimage,[4] using this faith in a process that leads to decisions about marriage, vocation, and the durabilities of friendships. This individualized belief system informs decisions about their physical lifestyle and facilitates their ability to experience and process a wide range of emotions in growth-producing fashion. It provides an overall context in which to think critically about a variety of topics, including faith itself.

Remember that late adolescents develop independence, either through rebellion or with their parents' blessings. They not only socialize apart from their family, they also live away from their family. In the West, socially acceptable ways of leaving the family include marriage, college, the military, and the pursuit of a job. In Asian societies, it is expected that young adults will stay in the parents' household and under the parents' authority for a longer number of years.

The failure to develop intellectual, economic, spiritual, and emotional independence will limit the young adult's capacity for social independence. There can be no refinement and consolidation of the social lifestyle until earlier issues have been settled. Seeking social independence apart from settling the other issues frequently leads to violent conflict between parents and their late-adolescent offspring. Late adolescents complain that their parents are still trying to run their lives while the parents bemoan the fact that their children are still dependent on them economically but desire too much freedom. Autonomy struggles dominate some late adolescents' concerns. However, without family support and an adequate foundation in early and middle adolescence, such autonomy is not likely to come.

Needs to Be Assessed in a Crisis

Older adolescents need a **faith system** that helps them interpret and make sense of the confusion and nonsense of their growing up. This includes sorting through and interpreting any sexual, physical, or emotional abuse from parents or others and winning the struggle for independence. They need large doses of the kinds of processes that began when they were younger. For example, they need a blessing from their parents like that received by Isaac and Jacob. They need to know that their parents affirm *who* they will become as well as their *right* to become. A young man named Brad sent his father a parable. The parable was of an Oriental son who came in silence and stood until his father blessed him. When the father refused to bless him, the son stood in silence for a day and a half. Finally, the father returned and gave his son a blessing that said, "Go where you must go. If you are right in your pursuit, come and inform me. If you are wrong, come and I will still love you." Brad sought such a blessing.

Older teens need the freedom to make mistakes. They need the freedom to pursue their own path as the father gave the prodigal his fair share and sent him on his way (Luke 15:11–32). Even with suspicions that trouble lay ahead, this freedom was granted. Such freedom enables growth for late adolescents. Similarly, as the father extended grace and forgiveness when the adolescent returned to beg a position as a servant, parents of older adolescents need to extend to them forgiveness and grace. Although the process of giving blessings, freedom, and forgiveness begins at the birth of the child, it reaches its highest point as the late adolescent prepares to leave the primary family system.

Developmental crises common in late adolescence focus around the three major tasks of developing an identity, deciding on a vocation, and forming intimate relationships with the opposite sex. Issues involving identity include choosing among finding a first job, enlisting in the military, enrolling for further training in vocational school or college or university, and getting married. The big identity question is caught up with these job, school, and marital decisions. They are closely interwoven. Who am I? Am I student or employee, single or married, and does the type of job fit my ideal self? There are so many possibilities that choice itself becomes a typical and frustrating late-adolescent crisis.

Both parents and adolescents experience trauma around any decision of moving out. There is the grief of leaving home and the anxiety of independent living, but also there is the joy of newfound freedom and the excitement of new places and new faces. Moving from home, behaviorally, is symbolic of the shift in the relationship with the parents. Authority shifts from the parents to the adolescent. However, new responsibilities accompany this freedom. These transition issues cluster to form the major developmental needs and crises of late adolescence.

Common **emergency crises** erupt, especially when developmental needs are not dealt with effectively. The three major emergencies involve pregnancy, legal issues, and substance abuse. However, minor crises can arise from illness or accident and unemployment.

Pregnancy is a crisis for late-adolescent males and females. Although there are alternatives, which involve decisions about abortion, marriage, adoption, or single parenthood, there are no easy choices for most teens and their families. Frequently conflicts of values between the generations add to the disruptive nature of a crisis of pregnancy.

Many late adolescents have their first encounter with the legal system through traffic violations—everything from parking tickets to driving under the influence of alcohol and reckless homicide. These are all crises of emergency proportions, and adolescents need the help of caring adults. They need guidance in the legal maze and in their emotional reactions, to identify potential learning and growth points. They need someone with whom to reflect.

A third area of major emergency crisis is substance abuse. Drug and alcohol abuse may start as excitement during early adolescence or through experimentation with other substances during middle adolescence, but it becomes a sick habit in late adolescence. Treatment programs are usually necessary for a late adolescent to completely kick a habit. While many large communities have such programs, facilities are seldom available in smaller communities for adequate inpatient substance-abuse treatment. A caring referral system, however, can provide information to the adolescent and his or her family. It is important that a caregiver assist these adolescents in reentry into the community after they leave an abuse program. Peer pressure is a major factor in beginning alcohol and drug abuse, and peer support is a major factor in recovery.

Minor crises such as illness, an accident, or unemployment create much anxiety when first experienced by an older adolescent trying freedom and independence. Although parents may wish to rescue them, it is best if parents and caregivers can remain in a supportive role and permit the older adolescent to handle as much of the crisis as possible. A danger exists that a minor crisis may halt the growth toward independence.

3

Principles of Caring

A young man had fallen asleep during the long-winded late-night preaching of the apostle Paul. Perched in a third-story window, Eutychus sank down with sleep and fell from the open window. Bystanders had taken him for dead, but Paul "bent over him, and embracing him said, 'Do not be alarmed, for his life is in him.' And when Paul had gone up and had broken bread and eaten, he conversed with them a long while, until daybreak, and so departed. And they took the lad away alive, and were not a little comforted."

This ancient story of Paul and Eutychus (Acts 20:7–12) illustrates what should happen in the religious care of an adolescent in crisis. First, Eutychus communicated his lack of appreciation for the traditional methods of adult education nonverbally by falling asleep during the lecture. Second, bystanders were quick to give up on him; they pronounced him dead and presumably returned to Paul for the important adult stuff. Third, turning from his preaching, Paul attended to the young man and embraced him. Fourth, Paul turned to the community to comfort them about the young man's condition. Fifth, Paul did not return to his preaching but stopped for a meal, and they all talked until the sun came up. And finally, they all celebrated to see new life in the young man

The principles of pastoral care and counseling with adolescents call for similar responses. While we might differ somewhat with Paul's methods, the approach is still sound.

Principles of pastoral care and counseling create a framework and a context in which to ground one's ministry. Principles provide a sense of direction in the maze of multifaceted problems that surround troubled adolescents. Furthermore, sound pastoral principles help maintain the unique identity and role of the pastoral caregiver as he or she interacts with other members of the therapeutic team. These principles assist in maintaining an overview and in looking at long-range goals in the face of the many intermediate issues that are involved in the ongoing care of an adolescent. The principles that follow are not discussed in order of their importance. They are to be taken together as a whole and viewed as the skeletal structure of an organism. Just as "the eye cannot say to the hand, 'I have no need of you' " (I Cor. 12:21), one principle cannot be rejected in favor of another. Nor are they intended to be all inclusive; they are suggested for you to examine and integrate into your own theoretical presuppositions and unique style of caring for adolescent persons. While there is a paradoxical side to several of these principles, I suggest they be held in dynamic tension to help maintain the strength of the total organism.

Relationship

The first set of principles focuses on the relationship between the minister and the adolescent, which is probably the essential factor in determining whether or not one can successfully nurture an adolescent through a time of crisis. Many descriptive terms get at the ideal nature of a helping relationship. However, all fall short of fully describing it. Friendship, as suggested by Wayne Oates in *The Christian Pastor*, is one of the first levels of pastoral care.[1] However, to shepherd an adolescent through a crisis, friendship is just the beginning. "Therapeutic alliance," the traditional medical and psychological term, speaks profoundly but, for a minister, may imply too much distance. In addition to appearing somewhat detached, it sometimes carries a mechanical connotation. "Minister-parishioner," when understood theologically, perhaps captures the nature of the relationship. However, adolescents find little meaning in such terms.

Many analogies have been used to describe the relationship—teacher, coach, counselor, doctor—yet all of them carry connotations that can serve as barriers to forming the relationship. Teens who showboat with their peers refer to a counselor as "my shrink."

In order to form a less threatening context for the adolescent, I suggest the terms "caring professional" and "professional friend." I often remind teens that while I'm a professional counselor I'm also their friend. This has the advantage of connoting both support through caring and friendship and responsibility or authority through the term "professional."

Whatever term is chosen, the nature of the relationship is all-important. In assessing relationships between caring professionals and adolescents that have been deemed somewhat successful from both sides, several factors emerge as consistently present.

Respect

Perhaps the most essential characteristic of the relationship is respect. The minister needs to be careful not to take adolescents and their problems lightly, not to belittle or talk down to adolescents, and never to negotiate around the adolescents when decisions are made about them. A healthy respect for teens must be reflected in the public context of teaching, preaching, and socializing with the congregation, long before it is uttered in a more formal counseling context.

Durability

A second characteristic of the relationship is durability. The professional friend needs to be able to form long term, dependable relationships with teenagers. Frequently troubled juveniles are detached from caring adults in their life, and perhaps always have been. Durability of relationship forms a bond that not only signals the importance of the adolescent as a person but aids the adolescent in managing anxieties from being alone in the world. Concrete ways of expressing the durability of the relationship involve such things as being certain that the next visit, appointment, or contact is defined before finishing a given dialogue, and continuing to stay abreast of the major developments in an adolescent's world. The pastor who has attended an eighth-grader's graduation ceremony and asked about adjustments to the first year of high school will find it easier to develop a durable relationship in any subsequent crisis. Likewise, a pastoral counselor who checks with the adolescent periodically concerning important events, such as a job interview or a date or a visit with a relative, signals the durability and ongoing nature of their relationship.

Flexibility

Flexibility, a third characteristic of the caring professional's relationship with adolescents, calls for meeting each adolescent where he or she is and modifying the therapeutic context to accommodate that person's situation. For example, many adolescents have difficulty being called into an office and sitting for the formal hour of counseling so characteristic of therapy. A flexible therapist can have meaningful conversations seated in a recreation lounge, sharing a soft drink, taking a walk, or simply standing and pacing around the room. Not only is flexibility needed in terms of the therapeutic context of the relationship, flexibility is important in terms of the emotional and psychological distance between the caregiver and the young person. While some teenagers respond positively to an open, warm, enthusiastic, caring professional, others will pull back in suspicion and fear. A caring professional also needs to be flexible over time, to move toward or away from attachments with the adolescent, depending on the adolescent's current needs. For example, after three months of fairly intensive counseling, an eighteen-year-old began to reveal intense anger toward his father and stepmother. As the pastoral counselor acknowledged that anger and facilitated its expression, he also communicated warmth and understanding. The young man failed to show up for the next appointment, and only after several weeks was he able to talk in an informal way about resuming the sessions. Three months later, however, he did return, explaining that he had felt anxious and frightened when the counseling got too involved. Time resolved this anxiety.

Understanding

A fourth characteristic of a caring professional's relationship with adolescents is understanding. Teenagers are more concerned that they be understood and heard than they are concerned that they be agreed with. In one therapeutic group setting, a fifteen-year-old girl said, "I wish adults knew what it was like to be a teenager just for one day!" Her forgetting that of course all adults have been teenagers seemed to indicate that the adults in her life had not used their experience or their professional insights to understand her. While every generation of adolescents faces a new world context with unique pressures, many problems remain the same. While a caring professional may not be able to say, "I know exactly what makes you afraid," he or she can say, "I remember being afraid when I first began dating."

Confidentiality

A fifth principle in the relationship between caring professionals and youth is confidentiality. While confidentiality is important in all ministry and counseling, it is crucial when dealing with adolescents because of legal issues involved when they are still minors. Adolescents need to know that their words are private, will be handled professionally, and will not be repeated lightly in conversations with parents and other helping persons. Adolescents who fail to receive a pledge of confidentiality do not trust helping persons. Very little progress can be made on the basis of such distrust. However, adolescents need to understand that if they become a threat to themselves or to other persons, the professional friend will have to intervene and communicate with parents and the professional community.

Sexual Transference

The final principle involving the relationship between caring professionals and teenagers involves an issue of sexuality. Male-female relationships and transference are certainly difficult issues in counseling people of all ages. However, because of the teenager's fragile sexual identity, sexual transference and countertransference issues are an even greater concern during adolescence. The adolescent needs to be reassured and to be able to feel comfortable, whether the caring professional is of the same sex or of the opposite sex. Ideally, male and female teams of caregivers will work with an adolescent in crisis. However, this is not always possible. Because of sexual transference issues, one must be extremely careful in touching and hugging a hurting adolescent. While there is a therapeutic place for touching and embracing, certainly this needs to be avoided in private settings and minimized even in public. Before one touches or embraces an adolescent, the previously mentioned principle of respect would demand that you ask permission. Since adolescents' emotions are likely to be vulnerable, especially in a time of crisis, one must be careful not to manipulate the adolescent in seeking such permission.

Also remember that transference-countertransference issues can be a difficulty in relation to the parent/child role. Caring professionals may be unconsciously tempted to treat adolescents as their own offspring. Such treatment, when outside the awareness of the caregiver, can be extremely dangerous for the caregiver's stability and for the adolescent's progress.

Assessment

A number of principles relate to the process of assessing the teenager, understanding the nature of the crisis, and determining the level of available support from the family and the community. Of course, traditional issues dealing with the nature of the crisis, the definition of the problem, the history of the individual and the family, the support system available, and the extent to which the crisis has impacted the individual and the family must be taken into account as in all professional counseling situations. As in other types of pastoral care and counseling, the minister primarily assesses from a theological perspective but is aware of the multifaceted dimensions of any crisis and seeks information from the teenager or from other professionals concerning psychosocial, educational, vocational, medical, legal, and family dynamics.

Developmental Stage

The first principle in assessing the issues facing an adolescent in crisis is to remember that one is dealing with an adolescent first and a crisis second. Normally we use our information concerning the nature of a crisis as the major template for assessment. However, with adolescents, the developmental stage of the adolescent's struggle becomes the major overlying factor in making the assessment. For example, in dealing with an adolescent girl whose mother had recently committed suicide, several professionals attempted to work with her in processing grief, but she continued to deteriorate; she pulled farther away from her family, became more involved in antisocial acting out, and even became suicidal herself. Initially, she did not seem interested in discussing either her family crisis, the issues surrounding her difficulties with the law, or her mother's suicide. She seemed preoccupied by a perceived injustice—having to live with her biological father and stepmother. As these issues were explored further, it became evident that her major sense of grief was the loss of a boyfriend in the high school she was forced to leave in order to move to her father's house. She felt guilty for being preoccupied with her boyfriend. Her family and other therapists had assumed that her "puppy love" was such a small issue in light of the other dynamics that it had been pushed aside. However, when she was able to address her grief over her boyfriend and to negotiate some opportunities to continue to see him, her depression lifted and she was able to deal rather predictably with her grief and her adjustment to a new school. More importantly, her acting out ceased and she was able to return to the tasks of seeking an education and getting on with life. The developmental need, dating and learning to relate to boys, was more significant than the grief process. This is not to say her mother was unimportant but that developmental issues are paramount in dealing with adolescents.

These developmental issues provide a tint to emergency crises. Since most crisis research has been done with adults, particularly grief work, the coloring added to the crisis by the adolescent's developmental issues needs to be taken more seriously and some thought given to adolescent grief or adolescent crisis response being different from the norms reported in research.

Facets of the Crisis

A second major assessment principle concerns the multifaceted dimension of adolescent crises. Few if any adolescents experience a crisis in one area only. The world of adolescents is an interconnected, interrelated entanglement of forces centering around their particular developmental stage, their social context, and their emotional, moral, and spiritual maturity.

Figure 3 shows how a matrix can be formed in looking at the various dynamics of the crisis. Each issue also has a forced dynamic affecting the whole. If pressure is put on one point, it pulls and distorts the entire matrix like a net tied of rubber bands. In assessing the nature of a crisis with an adolescent, therefore, one must gather information from a variety of sources. Educational information, medical information, psychological testing, social and family history, and faith stance all contribute to the picture from which the assessment must be made.

A very prominent young woman from a leading church in her community was referred for counseling because she refused to go off to college, choosing instead what her professional parents thought was a menial job waiting on tables in a popular but not elegant restaurant. After several frustrating sessions, psychological testing revealed that the young woman's IQ was below average and she was not suited for college. When informed of these results, she was not surprised and confessed that she had cheated on exams and bought reports and term papers for all four years of high school. She was so guilt-ridden she could not continue. But she was unable to confess to her parents that she knew she was not college material. Her parents had always told her she could be anything she wanted to be if she tried hard enough. She knew it was not true, but she did not want to disappoint them for fear they would reject her. She chose to deal with their anger at her rebellion rather than with the shame of feeling she was unacceptable to them. Without the family history and psychological testing, the break-

Figure 3. Facets of an adolescent crisis.

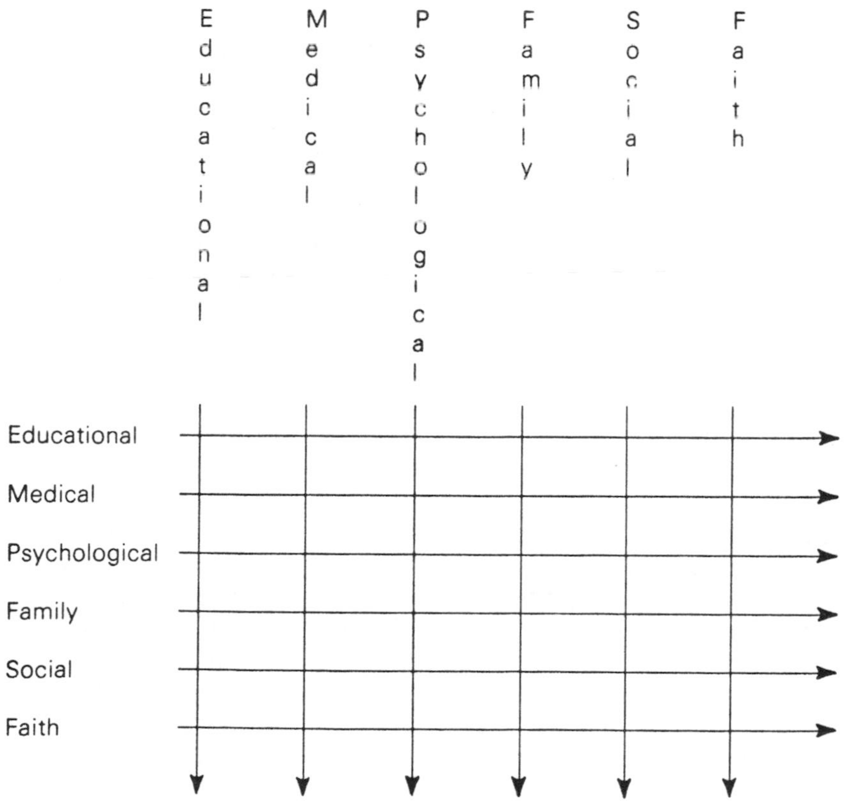
Educational
Medical
Psychological
Family
Social
Faith
Educational
Medical
Psychological
Family
Social
Faith

through in the assessment of this adolescent would have been nearly impossible. More so than with adults, adolescent counseling must involve the family background. This means not only the parent(s) and siblings living at home but the extended family of grandparents, aunts and uncles, stepparents, stepbrothers, and stepsisters. Also, in a family history the adolescent's perceptions of a relationship need to be assessed apart from the information given by other family members. The adolescent lives by his or her own perceptions, not the conclusions of others.

Likewise, consideration of social involvement in peer relationships is a significant part of dealing with teenagers. Because of the influence, particularly on middle and late adolescents, exerted by the peer group, the nature of the peer group must be clearly understood. The absence of a peer group signals a poor prognosis for quick and easy resolution of many crises.

Faith Development

Religious ideation of adolescents needs to be assessed in relationship to adolescent religious issues, not those of adults or children. In his popular book, *The Stages of Faith,* James Fowler has suggested that adolescent religion is primarily "stage 3," a synthetic conventional faith.[2] This stage is characterized by early formal operations as a form of logic. Teens can think in the abstract using symbols and propositions to work out alternative solutions to problems. They see the "gray" issues between the light and dark poles. They have a mutual interpersonal perspective on relationships. They can look at relationships from other people's points of view. An interpersonal expectations form of logic helps them to focus on doing what is right in the eyes of their authority figures and in their own eyes. Their group (peers' and parents' social class) serves as a bond of social awareness. They see primarily the social issues of only their group. Group consensus is an external locus of authority. If their group says a thing is right, they are relatively powerless to think for themselves and resist that position. "Everybody is doing it" is a basis for authority. Felt meanings become a form of world coherence. Their experience of life is defended uncritically as "the way life is for others." Teens find evocative power in multidimensional symbols. Their symbols are not separated from what the symbols stand for. Symbols, like a cross pendant, are powerful and will be defended against any reinterpretation.[3]

Randy Simmons demonstrates that the modal community of faith was a major factor in the adolescent's development according to the Fowler categories. The "general stage of faith in the community carried over to teens. In churches and faith communities where individuative reflective faith (stage 4) was normative, adolescents could also become stage four faith persons."[4] Because the minister will frequently share in the adolescent's faith system, it might be difficult to see how faith issues can block psychosocial development or how faith issues can serve to nurture and promote growth through resolving the crisis. Religious issues that frequently arise in crises with youth are the adolescent's concept of authority, the adolescent's stage of moral development, the adolescent's value system, and the adolescent's understanding of goodness and evil, of sin and forgiveness, and of one's own relationship to God.

Environmental Controls

A further assessment principle is to assess the nature of controls and limits in the adolescent's environment. Who and what determines the adolescent's behavior? While teenagers need freedom, they also need limits. Paradoxically, they need a balance between the two that provides a structure where expectations are clarified and routine and schedule are provided. They need enough structure to control their anxiety but enough freedom to permit their self-development. The family, the school, outside activities, the law, the use of time—all are important ingredients in assessing the structural context of the adolescent's world. E. Mansell Pattison argues that "religious youth cults are an alternative family structure for youth who find themselves lacking a viable family structure."[5]

Treatment

The main discussion of treatment principles for caring professionals with adolescents in crisis appears under methods of intervention in chapter 4, but a few will be highlighted here.

Make Referrals

First, know and respect your own limits and refer teenagers to other professionals when wisdom dictates. The crisis may call for expertise beyond your training or may demand more time than you can realistically offer. The adolescent may hook you in a positive or a negative manner. Don't play Lone Ranger and neglect other members of the caring team. When making a referral, do so in a clear, direct, and caring fashion that avoids rejection. Explain why and to whom you are making the referral. Then follow up in a short period of time to see how the referral process unfolded. Show that you still care.

Know the Teenagers' Worldview

Second, understand and use adolescent symbols and concepts of reality in communicating with them. This involves more than understanding their jargon and in phrases. It is more than knowing their favorite type of clothing, rock group, or slang language. One needs to know how a given adolescent comprehends the world. Discover how concrete and how informal or abstract the young person is when trying to gather and process information. One must be careful not to be lulled into thinking or acting like an adolescent; one must maintain an adult perspective. Understand their worldview, but remain squarely in touch with your own.

Listen Carefully

A third principle of counseling adolescents in a time of crisis is to *listen, listen, and listen.* Patience in listening to adolescents often requires the regular therapeutic 50-minute hour to be modified to include a number of briefer sessions or a few extended ones. At times there is a need for seemingly marathon sessions, where the adolescent, especially early in counseling, is permitted to talk through the confusion surrounding the crisis. Sometimes this will not be at convenient times; some adolescents seem to function better in the late evening. As we listen, we need to hear not only the thoughts and the content of the conversation but, more importantly, the affective responses to events. Listen for clues to the decisions and intentions about their behavior in light of both thoughts and feelings. Secret plans are revealed in language designed to reach out for help. Listen in a way that will assist them in understanding how their thoughts and feelings affect their behavior and how they can be responsible for their thoughts, aware of their feelings, and therefore responsible for their own behavior. Don't be afraid to follow clues and hints as you read between the lines. Listen to what the words imply.

Collaborate in Decisions

A fourth treatment principle involves collaborating in the growth task. One cannot tell adolescents what to do and expect instant change. However, one can teach adolescents when they ask. Collaborating with adolescents means that they are ultimately responsible for their growth. They understand that what happens to them is primarily their own responsibility. Helping them accept responsibility for themselves strengthens the helping professional's therapeutic process.

A fifth treatment principle concerns making meaning out of life and life's events. As an adolescent tells his or her story in relationship to the gospel story (or to the songs, poems, books, or movies that make up the symbolic belief system), the caregiver can interpret, reflect, and facilitate new ways of thinking about the world. Since many adolescents in modern society will be ignorant of the gospel story, some teaching may be necessary. However, songs, literature, movies, and adolescent folklore can be used to assist the adolescent to find meaning in life.

Deal with Anger

A final principle deals with the approach to anger in the discussions. Adolescents carry a lot of anger. They are volatile or sullen, depending on whether they externalize or internalize their feelings. The ability to receive an adolescent's anger without being hooked into an escalation or mutual put-down session is a very important part of the therapeutic context. The caring professional is able to facilitate a juvenile's expression of anger and is careful not to attack personally but to set firm, caring limits. One such counselor repeatedly reminds teens, "I know what I am saying must frustrate you. I hope you will learn to deal with it." Because of the fragile nature of the adolescent's identity in the context of the crisis, anger can be spurred by simple misunderstandings and by jumping to conclusions on the basis of limited information. Before facilitating the constructive expression of anger with teens, evaluate the data and check the validity of the basis for the anger.

One concluding reflection on the context of pastoral care and counseling with adolescents in crisis sums up the stance that leads to effective intervention. Ministers who venture into caring for persons in crisis know that three elements surpass the others: faith, hope, and love. "The greatest of these is love" (I Cor. 13:13b). With teenagers this is even more true, because they are in life's major transition period. They are no longer caterpillars and not yet butterflies. You who reach out to them must have an extra capacity to love them.

4

Methods for Pastoral Care and Counseling

Methods of dealing with adolescents in crisis vary widely among personality theorists and among approaches to psychotherapy. For a detailed discussion of contemporary methods of pastoral counseling, see Howard Clinebell's *Basic Types of Pastoral Care and Counseling*. Most counseling methods need to be adjusted when used with teenagers. The principles in chapter 3 provide the framework for such adjustments. We now examine interviewing methods, crisis intervention and problem-solving methods, pastoral psychotherapy (including behavioral and cognitive approaches with teens, meditation and relaxation, family counseling, and transactional analysis) and pastoral care responses.

Interviewing

In interviewing adolescents, traditional interpersonal factors are especially important. Significant consideration must be given to displaying nonpossessive warmth, interpersonal integrity, and an open, aboveboard approach. The ability to empathize is crucial for counseling troubled adolescents because many of these youngsters maintain a generalized suspicion of and rebellion against such adult authority figures as ministers and counselors. As one depressed high school senior said, "I will never spill my guts to any counselor or shrink or whatever It's like talking to the principal."

When interviewing adolescents, more time than usual needs to be spent in clearly introducing yourself, your role in this particular context, and your function as seen by the adolescent. Until the adolescent knows, understands, and trusts you and your approach, very little productive counseling can take place. Adolescents appear to be more comfortable when they have something to offer in the relationship and are not merely seen as counselees. I found that adolescent resistance was not nearly so high when I told them I was also conducting research and would be interested in their comments, advice to parents, and tips for other counselors. Offering a role with dignity and power significantly reduced the resistance in several instances. Take time to build a trusting relationship. If parents grow impatient that the process isn't moving faster, provide reassurance.

As soon as the contract for counseling has been clarified and the relationship formulated, the major interviewing time concentrates on facilitating the adolescent's discussion of the problem. It is time to listen and to listen intently. Exploratory questions, like those introduced by Norm Kagan in his *Interpersonal Process Recall,* are essential interviewing tools for adolescents.[1] Gerard Egan in *The Skilled Helper* likewise provides excellent information on getting at the crisis.

Reframing the problem, clarifying significant and less significant issues, and looking at events from various perspectives are important interviewing techniques with adolescents. Reframing the problem helps the adolescent to focus on the central causative issues and move away from preoccupations with relatively insignificant matters. Distinguishing foreground from background helps the adolescent to focus on the issues in a crisis more clearly. To discover patterns and to understand relationship in a different light strengthens the young person's hope for progress.

The final interviewing issue with adolescents also originates from their concern for trusting relationships. Adolescents appreciate the opportunity to ask questions as you clarify your continued role and your future relationship with them. Adolescents need a concrete commitment as to when and how you will be in contact. Clear up any questions about phoning you as they need.

Generally speaking, one must be more deliberate, direct, and in control when interviewing an adolescent. This is not to imply that one can get away with speaking down to or overpowering adolescents, but that one must be very conscious of taking responsibility for the flow and direction of the counseling.

Crisis Intervention and Problem-solving

Initially there will be a presenting problem or crisis that has brought the adolescent to the attention of the institution or into your professional care. Occasionally an institution will make the referral, such as in court-ordered counseling; more often the parents will make the contact; only occasionally will the adolescent in crisis have enough initiative and ego strength to initiate counseling plans personally. A minister who is regularly around the adolescent in an informal setting can often formalize counseling sessions when problems and crises are being discussed. Suggesting a more formal setting helps the adolescent feel hopeful. Also, being taken seriously tells the adolescent that he or she is important to the minister. Basic problem-solving intervention with adolescents has a few modifications from adult crisis intervention. However, the overall process is quite similar.

Defining the Problem

The first phase is defining the problem from various perspectives and contracting for ongoing counseling intervention. In working with adolescents, more so than with the normal adult population, one will need to check out the facts as the story of the crisis unfolds; not that adolescents always deliberately misrepresent the facts, although some will. Their perception and understanding of the adult world are noticeably limited. If there are legal implications to their difficulty, a maze of misinformation may need to be checked out. One can validate the facts and perceptions by contacting other institutions and other parties involved and by talking with parents. Let the young person know you intend to verify your understanding of the crisis.

Also, in defining the problem it is important to clarify the goals and values of the adolescent in relation to those of the family, school, and perhaps church. The adolescent may see the problem as not enough freedom and time for fun, while the parents see the problem as not enough application to schoolwork. The school report may support or refute either or both. Unclear expectations and commitments to common goals could be the common denominator. Until the problem is clarified, no problem-solving methods can be successfully employed.

Theological dynamics most at work in defining the problem are assessing guilt, sorting out the truth, and giving and receiving forgiveness. Much blaming during the definition of the problem will involve projections from parents and adolescents as well as peers and other adults. Sorting through the story so all concerned can accept responsibility for their own mistakes can lead to authentic forgiveness and reconciliation.

Thinking of Alternatives

Hope sets the context for the second phase of crisis and problem-solving intervention with adolescents. Only hope permits one to think of alternatives. Basically, alternatives fall into three categories: adaptation of self and environment, acceptance of self and environment, and avoidance of self and environment. Adaptation involves ways of changing thoughts, attitudes, behaviors, feelings, and beliefs. Acceptance involves alternatives that change the guidelines, rules, and expectations for the relationships; one learns to live with life as it is. Avoidance involves alternatives that change the living structures. In avoidance, for example, out-of-home placements with institutions, foster families, or relatives would be primary considerations.

A commitment on the part of the adolescent and the family toward a common goal comes before the defining of alternatives. If either the family or the adolescent refuses to look at common alternatives, there may be a need for legal and institutional intervention. For example, a minor adolescent may need assistance in filing a petition for state care if the parents are essentially throwing their child out on the street. The parent may need to file an out-of-control petition if the adolescent has a character disorder and absolutely refuses to look at responsible alternatives.

After a wide variety of alternatives are mutually suggested by the adolescent and the family, the counselor can move to informing them about any other possibilities. In the ministry of informing, the counselor needs to be cautious not to regress to simple advice giving but to be satisfied with providing the information necessary for other alternatives to be understood.

Evaluating the Alternatives

The third phase of crisis and problem-solving counseling is evaluating the alternatives. This involves not only each person's spontaneous emotional reaction but some serious gathering of data and projecting the possible outcomes of each alternative. The impact will differ for each person. The freedom and openness given by God to all humanity models the attitude for listening and evaluating alternatives with respect for each individual's position. Frustrated parents may find it difficult to treat their adolescent with dignity and freedom, and at this point the counselor may need to side with the adolescent in a way that acknowledges her or him as still a person of worth. However, at other times the counselor may need to support the parents in persuading the adolescent to look responsibly at the evaluation of the alternatives.

In evaluating the alternatives, it is important to remember that adolescents' time perspectives, values, and needs differ greatly from those of their parents. Teens value here-and-now issues and view a year as a much longer time than do adults. Creating in advance the expectations for both parents and adolescents that their alternatives will be radically different assists in reducing the shock and tension when they are discussed.

The process of making decisions is not usually well formulated for adolescents. Guiding is a pastoral perspective for this step. Draw out their resources for making evaluations. They may need assistance in learning to list positive and negative potential outcomes where thoughts, meanings, feelings, and behaviors are taken into consideration. Otherwise, adolescents are likely to make a decision based on what feels good from a short-term perspective. This is especially true of adolescents who are still bewildered and confused in the early phases of a crisis.

Deciding on a Plan

After ample evaluation of alternatives the fourth phase of counseling, deciding on a mutually acceptable alternative, brings some resolution and relief of pent-up emotions. While making the decisions may be difficult and involve open confrontation and differences, after the decisions are made comes a general sense of relief and excitement. During the time of decision-making, the theological dynamics of guiding are paramount. As a sense of celebration and joy are shared, one must be careful not to substitute deciding for the actual implementation of the decision. Reconciliation may be needed before any mutual decision can be discussed

Implementing the Plan

The fifth phase of problem-solving counseling with adolescents focuses on planning the implementation of the decision. Specific responsibilities for implementing the plan are allocated by the adolescent and other involved persons.

Planning the implementation will be greatly limited by the adolescent's lack of experience in the adult world. You may need to provide information about resources and institutions that can assist in planning the implementation. The adolescent needs a clear, probably written list of his or her responsibilities in the plan. Likewise, the parents should make a clear statement of their responsibilities.

It is especially important for adolescents to have regular reinforcement during the trial period of their crisis-resolution plans. The contact itself and phones, letters, and visits will facilitate their continued commitment to living by the process. They need to be sustained.

Whatever the plan, there can be a time of celebration and joy and an asking of God's strength and blessings for the decisions. Isaiah 40:28–31 has been helpful for some adolescents and parents because it reminds everyone that they are dependent on a power greater than themselves. Their willingness to confess that fact seems to be a critical factor in the success of working through any crisis, but especially addictions.

Reevaluating the Plan's Effectiveness

The final phase is reevaluating the effectiveness of the plan. Regular checkup periods encourage everyone to resolve the crisis. This process serves as behavioral reinforcement for both the parents and the adolescent. Also, it symbolizes ongoing sustaining from the pastoral counselor toward the individuals and the system at large. In the checkup sessions new issues will undoubtedly suggest some necessary mid-course corrections. A process similar to that used in initially selecting the plan may be necessary to resolve new issues that surface. Mid-course corrections are defined in terms of their problem and the alternatives generated, evaluated, selected, planned for, and tried. Furthermore, in the periodic report sessions, an important function for the counselor in offering hope is to summarize progress. The counselor reminds both adolescent and adults of what progress has been made. This plays no small part in encouraging movement toward healing and wholeness.

Pastoral Psychotherapy

Adolescents and their families may need deeper levels of intervention than problem-solving can provide, to deal with self, family system, and worldviews. Pastoral psychotherapy, as the approach to counseling that integrates biblical and theological foundations with a particular school of psychotherapy, works best with adolescents when integrated with the approaches to therapy that research indicates are successful with young people. For the purposes of this study we will look at behavior modification, cognitive therapy, meditation, family systems, and transactional analysis.

Behavior Modification

Behavior modification is perhaps most successful in treating adolescents suffering from character disorders, substance abuse, or eating disorders. In establishing a behavior modification program, all authority persons related to the adolescent must be committed to and involved in supporting the program. If the adolescent might be institutionalized, all staff must work together for the program to be effective. If the adolescent lives with the family, parents, grandparents, teachers, and other authority persons working with them must understand and support the system. Adolescents can be particularly skilled at playing "divide and conquer," where they pit one authority person against another in an attempt to shirk responsibility.

In setting up a behavior modification program, several instructions are essential. First of all, the reward system must be something that the adolescent values. I often request a list of wishes and then set up rewards. While some rewards are gifts from parents, most are trips and the use of time for enjoyable activities. Second, there needs to be both long-term and short-term reinforcements. Small daily rewards can be steps toward a major reinforcement. Third, the program succeeds when paying attention to good behavior goes along with the token or reward. An honest compliment goes a long way. Finally, for adolescents the program is better when there is a combination of four types of responses in the behavior modification program. As seen in Figure 4, the responses are (1) turning on a positive, (2) turning off a positive, (3) turning on a negative and (4) turning off a negative. Turning on a positive creates pleasure or joy; for example, for good school grades some parents add a bonus to the allowance. Turning off a positive creates loss and grief; withholding phone privileges for poor grades also gives more time for study. Turning on a negative creates pain and motivates by fear; a coach makes a player run extra laps around the field. Turning off a negative creates relief and motivates by hope; a parent might say, "I helped you clean your room this week because you did such good work at school the past six weeks." Hope and joy are the two greatest motivators. However, they work best when they are interspersed with the loss of a positive and the fear of a negative.

**Figure 4. Four types of responses
in behavior modification.**

	ON	OFF
	(1)	(2)
Positive	Pleasure	Loss
Response	Joy	Grief
	(3)	(4)
Negative	Pain	Relief
Response	Fear	Hope

Regular reinforcement of consistent, clear expectations assists the adolescent in accepting ultimate responsibility for the outcome. The attitudes of the counselor and other authority persons working with the behavior modification system can be either "We are really pulling for you to do these things for yourself" or "We are sorry you chose not to do them and not to receive the rewards." The adults are careful not to let themselves be set up as doing something *to* the adolescent. The rewards and punishments are the adolescent's own choices by the behavior that he or she elects.

Cognitive Therapy

Cognitive therapy has an excellent record with assisting adolescents with depression and low self-esteem [2] In combination with behavior modification, cognitive therapy shows promise for several other issues, such as eating disorders and distorted thinking.[3] Depression seems to grow worse through a vicious cycle of affecting the teenager's inability accurately to evaluate input from peers and the environment. The teenager becomes negative about self, about the environment, and about the future. This produces a lack of hope and a negative self-image that leads to negative feelings and further depression. Cognitive therapy rests on the assumption that the process of acquiring knowledge and forming beliefs primarily determines one's mood and therefore one's behavior.[4] If one thinks one is unacceptable, others do not care, and there is no hope to change, feelings of depression follow and behaviors associated with depression—such as lack of motivation, failure to stay with a task, and inability to concentrate—are natural outcomes. The major thrust of cognitive therapy is to identify and correct negative, distorted information processes. Several cognitive errors are traditional with adolescents.[5] (See *Feeling Good* by David Burns for how self-defeating thoughts can lead to self-defeating feelings which bring self-defeating actions.) Because of the pastoral counselor's ability to deal realistically with hope, the hopelessness of this cycle can be broken. Alternatives for overcoming the depression are not limited to rethinking the data. While distortions play a major role in teenage depression, these young people do experience some real-life loss and grief.

Typical adolescent thought patterns include helplessness, the "nobody can do anything about this anyway" kind of thinking. All-or-nothing thinking, also typical of adolescents in crisis, is demonstrated in such statements as "If I can't have everything my way, I just won't take anything." A third typical distortion is the always-and-never type of thinking; "it is never going to be any better" and "I am always going to be this way" are obvious expressions of this hopelessness.

The first task is to identify the automatic negative thinking behind the depressive emotions. Adolescents may not use the word "depression" to describe themselves but may simply say they are bored, tired, feel worthless, and generally don't want to do anything. As the automatic negative thoughts unfold, the counselor and the adolescent examine them in light of the evidence. Adolescents can be assigned a number of homework tasks to assist in confronting the fallacy of the negative thought. For example, they can keep a list of their automatic thoughts and then a list of what actually happens later in the day. They might think, as they get up in the morning, "Nothing good will happen today," but later that day as they keep their journal they will notice several positive things. The record of positives confronts the fallacy of the negative thoughts. A mastery and pleasure scale also confronts negative thinking. The adolescent keeps a list of activities and rates them from one to ten to show how well he or she did on the activity and how much fun it was. These records are then used to confront their negative thoughts about those activities. Negative cognitions set the adolescent up for feeling depressed. Reality testing assists the adolescent in moving out of the depression and into some sense of pleasure, joy, and hope. From a pastoral point of view the adolescent can be challenged that ultimately hope comes not from one's own strength but from one's awareness of being created in the image of God and having the redemptive process worked out in one's life.

Cognitive therapy is particularly helpful with adolescents who in their depression refuse to enter the counseling process and resist the formation of a therapeutic alliance.[6] Cognitive therapy helps adolescents to think more accurately about themselves, their environment, and their future, and as thought distortions are corrected, depression and hopelessness are replaced by hope and a corresponding sense of joy. Hope and joy bring a resulting willingness to join in the counseling process. Productive actions and behavior in turn generate new hope and joy. As in behavioral therapy with adolescents, this cognitive approach is dependent on regular brief periods of reinforcement between the counselor and the adolescent.

Adolescents sometimes develop a negative schema—a basic approach for screening, sorting, and evaluating data that is maladaptive. The schema might be something like: "If I don't have a boyfriend or a girlfriend, I am a nerd or dork." As long as they live by that basic schema, they are setting themselves up for depression. Uncovering cognitive distortions is much easier than uncovering negative schemata.[7] The schema serves as a premise for interpreting the events of life

Meditation

A third basic method with adolescents is the use of meditation. Adolescents can be taught methods of systematic desensitization and meditation. Their experimenting style of life makes new experiences easy to introduce. After they relax their bodies, they focus their thoughts on a word like hope, love, or joy. Then they pray about their major anxieties or imagine facing a feared activity such as returning to school. Adolescents who suffer from anxiety are particularly encouraged by this approach. It gives them a sense of power and self-control because they feel they have a contact with power beyond themselves. Also, it gives them the ability to bring a sense of peace and quiet to their lives which displaces the anxiety feelings. Opposites cannot dominate the same space at the same time. It is important in this process when the negative feelings are overpowered to then turn the adolescent to a program of meditation and planning that will bring positive feelings. When the evil demons are cast out, the good spirits must take their place. For fifteen years I have used the meditation and relaxation approach with anxious adolescents with remarkable success.

One adolescent was incapable of attending her school classes and performing such routine tasks as going to the grocery store. With the assistance of relaxation and meditation techniques, she not only returned to a basic level of functioning but was able to graduate from high school and college.

Family Systems

Ministers regularly counsel families and are probably most used to family counseling approaches to psychotherapy. However, family counseling theorists present different pictures of what family therapy is. Some emphasize family history and feelings, others stress current structure and boundaries, while still others underscore the significance of communication strategies. Yet all share a view of the family as a system.[8] Rather than seeing events through an individual adolescent's set of assumptions, beliefs, feelings, thoughts, and behavioral patterns, the family counselor seeks to understand the crisis from the multiple perspectives of all members of the family system and to conceptualize the relationship between the patterns of interactions in that system and the crisis events. One asks, "How does this family's system affect the crisis?" and "How does this crisis impact the family?"

In counseling with teens and their families for two decades, I have come to rely on several key ingredients of a family's relationships for insights into the interrelatedness between the crisis and the family system. The **structure of the family unit** captures first attention. Who lives with the adolescent, and how are they related? Does this youngster have sufficient family structure to provide the physical and emotional nurture for growing up? The **open or closed nature** of the system is a second key issue. How does the nuclear family relate to its extended members, the neighbors, and the community (school, church, business, etc.)? How much interchange of ideas, support, and resources can be tolerated? Does the family have sufficient boundaries to define its own identity? **Communication patterns** and depths among family members and with the counselor arises as a third concern. Can members speak for themselves? Do they discuss only the basics of living together (food, shelter, time) or can they include ideas, emotions, dreams? What topics get ignored? **Conflict resolution methods** deserve detailed attention. Who has the family power and what is the method of using it? Who and how many participate in discussions about differences of opinions, varied expectations, and family resources? Are the *rules* clear and consistent and open for change as the children mature? What rules apply and to whom? Another concern is the **clarity of the roles** played by the parents and the offspring. Can wife and husband keep their relationship clear without entwining the roles of mother and father? Is any child expected to function in a parent role? One last issue, by no means least, regards the giving and receiving of appropriate **affirmation** among family members. Can the parents affirm each other's ego and sustain the marriage, or at least refrain from involving the children in their attacks? When parents are divorced, they should still communicate mutual respect in front of the children. Can parents give an honest compliment (a verbal blessing) to their sons and daughters?

A full discussion of the many methods of family intervention seems impractical here. Basically, the counselor becomes an adopted member of the family system and by identification with weaker members of the family restores some sense of homeostasis. By modeling effective communication methods, positive conflict-resolutions approaches, and warm respect for each person, a caring professional can significantly influence the family. Jay Haley focuses primarily on changing behavior patterns.[9] Nathan Ackerman's major concerns are to expose and resolve the family's conflicts and then to aid in maintaining its balance.[10] Murray Bowen's chief goal is the self-differentiation of each individual within the relationship.[11]

Family issues receive repeated attention in the Bible. From the creation accounts in Genesis to the household code of Paul in Ephesians, the scriptures affirm the role and power of family life. As will be seen in the next chapter, pastoral counselors can make a major contribution to adolescents and their families in crisis.

Transactional Analysis

Transactional analysis (TA) is an especially effective method for pastoral counseling because it uses a system of self-understanding (parent, adult, child)[12] that is easily communicated to adolescents.

The child ego state acts on the basis of "I feel" and begins at birth. A parent ego message is "I should" or "I should not" and is collected by the child from parents and authority figures. Adult ego messages begin around puberty and are the "I think" statements. They reflect the ability to decide the pros and cons of an issue and to act on what one thinks, not the "feel" or "should" impulses. Adolescents readily understand the communication theories of transactional analysis and respond positively to the concepts of games and scripts. Parallel transactions, crossed transactions, and ulterior transactions help them sort out their own communication problems. Figure 5 illustrates each.

**Figure 5. The three transactions
of Transactional Analysis.**

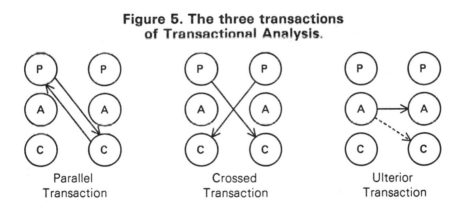

| Parallel | Crossed | Ulterior |
| Transaction | Transaction | Transaction |

A parallel transaction could be "You should know better" (parent to child) and "Yes, I really am sorry" (child to parent). A crossed transaction could be "You should know better" (parent to child) and "Who are you to tell me what I should know? You shouldn't talk to me that way" (parent to child). An ulterior transaction could be "Would you like to see my room?" (adult to adult), said in a tone that implies "Let's mess around" (child to child). A game is an unconscious interchange between two persons with an emotional payoff for the originater. For example, a teenager who flirts and then gets angry at the response is playing a game. A script is a belief that was learned early and controls one's life. One teen confessed, "I'm never going to amount to much; no one in my family does." Teens need to understand the unconscious nature of games and scripts so as not to feel needless shame and guilt. *Game Free* by Thomas Oden provides useful theological dialogue with the basic tenets of TA.[13]

Other Interventions

Many other methods of intervention are helpful with adolescents. Adolescents respond well in **group counseling**. Drama therapy can do for adolescents what play therapy does for children. The use of music in dealing with adolescents is helpful to assist not only in ventilation but also in establishing a common vocabulary and in understanding the adolescent's values. **Music and drama** can be listened to, written, discussed, and performed as a part of the therapy with adolescents. Likewise, **art therapy** is effective; adolescents who have difficulty verbalizing and participating in traditional forms of psychotherapy can often be reached with art. In working with adolescents, drama, music, and art all need to be used in conjunction with other approaches to counseling.

An effective method of intervention in any approach with youths is the use of **homework and journaling**. Because adolescents frequently keep a diary and regularly expect to do homework, the caring professional can be creative with a variety of methods of assigning tasks. Asking if it would be possible to see the diaries kept by an adolescent for a number of years might provide an excellent assessment tool (but make special efforts to maintain the confidentiality of these private reflections). Requesting that the adolescent write a personal song or a poem or a short story is frequently helpful. Suggesting that the adolescent make a list of the positive and negative possibilities about a given behavior or desired activity can also be helpful. Reading assignments that will assist the adolescent in self-understanding, understanding personality theory, or even understanding the basic principles of an approach to counseling might be productive.

Psychological testing with adolescents needs to be a reg
ular part of the treatment process because they are changing

so rapidly. Psychological testing provides useful cognitive and personality information as it assists in understanding the progress the adolescent has made in the developmental process. Testing instruments will vary from psychologist to psychologist, but pastoral counselors need to have a good working relationship with a psychologist who can test and evaluate adolescents and assist in making therapeutic suggestions. If one is not familiar with a given approach in pastoral psychotherapy, additional supervision and consultation are suggested. Reading a book and trying a new approach can be exciting, but a counselor's effectiveness will be greatly increased by careful, reflective case discussions with other counselors and supervisors.

Pastoral Care Responses

For centuries, ministers of the gospel have used certain unique resources and approaches to helping persons. They are still very effective methods of helping adolescents. When used carefully, prayer, Bible study, and religious dialogue all can contribute to the adolescent's response to a crisis.

Prayer

Adolescents in crisis can be asked if they pray and what they pray for. This will give the professional friend not only an insight into their anxiety and concerns but also an awareness of their concept of God and of authority persons. Many modern adolescents seem to have a preoccupation with spiritual matters and even a hunger for such involvement. The many religious groups of the 1970s and 1980s composed primarily of young people are a testimony to the attraction of adolescents for religious issues. Psychiatrist E. Mansell Pattison has written that the current rise of supernaturalism—belief in demonology, possession, exorcism—results from dissatisfaction with the Western scientific worldview, a lack of trust in social structures, and a mood of hopelessness.[14]

The use of prayer in the session can be introduced by asking "Is it OK if we pray?" and then developed by asking what the adolescent would like to have included in the prayer. It is helpful to give the adolescent time to pray. The counselor may wish to summarize the major themes and to seek God's guidance for the task ahead in his or her own prayer time. Explain that you will be praying for the adolescent at times other than in your sessions.

Bible Study

While adolescents who have participated regularly in formal Bible study will be familiar with the great themes, stories, and general theology of the scripture, most adolescents of this decade are uninformed concerning the Bible. Projective questions,[15] which provide the opportunity to name a favorite biblical character, story, or truth can assist not only in understanding the adolescent's level of religious and spiritual development but also in understanding his or her priorities and self-concept. While Bible study can be helpful in the formal context of Bible teaching, I have found the most effective use of Bible study for adolescents is in placing the great stories of scripture that teach values and responsibilities in a contemporary setting. Many times a role play or drama of a Bible story can be set up by a counselor in a group context so the adolescents can act out the biblical story and then discuss its meaning. These events are designed to facilitate moral development as well as to assist the adolescent in self-understanding and in empathizing with other persons.

Furthermore, as adolescents tell their own life stories, great stories of the scripture can be shared: for example, the accounts of David and Jonathan, of when Jesus chose to stay in the Temple, or of Timothy, the teenage missionary.

Religious Dialogue

Theological discussion provides an opportunity to talk with adolescents about their own presuppositions as to the role of God, the church, and others in their crisis or in their own perception of self. Adolescents need an opportunity to explore and examine their personal beliefs about God, the universe, personhood, and the way persons relate to God. Many times at the basis of a crisis is an unspoken and unexamined belief. For example, one young woman who had been molested by a teacher was unwilling to go back to school and unable to function, even after being released from a psychiatric setting. She maintained only that she was not blaming the teacher; then, after several sessions, she was able to say that she blamed God, because God had put the sexual appetite in the man who had molested her. In study and understanding she came to see that God does not control and manipulate persons and that it was not God's intention for men to sexually molest teenage girls. With that insight and understanding she was soon able to return to church, finding social interaction much less threatening. Now she can believe that she lives not in a universe where God wills that teenage girls be sexually molested, but in a world where God's will is much more loving.

In working with adolescents it is particularly helpful to avoid being drawn into theological arguments. Ultimately information can be shared, dialogue processed, and experiences pointed out, but the adolescent will have to discover his or her own faith system. A caring counselor points the way and encourages the faith journey.

5

Family Problems

All families can be expected to experience crises from time to time. A crisis exists when demands upon a family equal or exceed its resources. Usually a crisis is precipitated by a unique event such as illness, loss of job, or unmet financial expectations. However, for a family with adolescents, these youngsters' rapid changes produce a seemingly unending state of crisis. As adolescents think for themselves and move to declare independence through a personalized self-identity, all but the most gifted families will experience some upheaval. Recall that a crisis was precipitated for the parents of Jesus when they learned he had not traveled with them on the return trip from Jerusalem. After three days of searching, they found him in the Temple. His mother's words as recorded by Luke 2:48 are, "Son, why have you treated us so? Behold, your father and I have been looking for you anxiously." The early adolescent Jesus speaks to them about pursuing his own mission and asks, "Did you not know that I must be in my Father's house?" They do not understand, but he returns with them to Nazareth.

The reciprocal nature of the parent-child relationship is recorded in Ephesians 5 and 6. Ephesians 5:21, "Be subject to one another out of reverence for Christ," sets the foundation for understanding 6:1–4. The responsibility of children is to obey, honor, and respect their parents. There is also a responsibility of parents to nurture and discipline with such caring that they do not provoke children to anger. Maintaining the reciprocal nature of adolescent-parent relationships greatly facilitates crisis intervention at all levels. The assessment level begins by looking at both parental and adolescent issues. Seeking alternatives becomes a responsibility of both parents and adolescents. Counseling and care focuses on the adolescent and parents and on the family as a unit greater than the sum of its parts. This chapter will examine family dynamics in a crisis context, family stressors, and family resources.

Family Dynamics

Any discussion of family dynamics depends on basic assumptions about the nature of personhood and the point of view of the professional in approaching the family. From a pastoral care and counseling point of view, we will look at three components of family dynamics as they impact family identity struggle. These three—family covenants, calling, and centeredness—affect the individual, the marriage, and the family identity. Adolescents and their families who have a sense of mutual covenant, common calling, and personal centeredness in faith have resources for facing crises and solving them in ways that produce growth, not only for the individuals but within the system. Adolescents who lack a sense of covenant, calling, or centeredness not only experience more crises but also have fewer resources for coping.

The Identity Triangle

The identity triangle was first introduced in the family systems theory by Nathan Ackerman.[1] It strives to create reciprocality and homeostasis in the identities by maintaining a balance between the identity of the self, the identity of the marital pair, and the identity of the family (see Figure 6). Individual identity or self-concept constitutes the answer to the question "Who am I?" It includes body image, role definition, personality styles, and whatever else makes up one's self-definition. A youth said, "I'm a fifteen-year-old boy who enjoys sports, likes girls, hates school, and tolerates my family and delivering papers." The identity of the marital pair focuses on the blending of the husband's and wife's identities into their style of marriage relationship. The boy's parents reported, "We are a typical yuppie couple who have all we basically need, but we have lost contact with our son." Family identity passes from generation to generation and carries the family's self-concept and community image. The boy's father complained, "What would people in my hometown think if they knew a Newton had been in trouble with the juvenile authorities? Why, we are the foundation of the church!"

The three most significant dynamics for a family in maintaining its resources in the face of a crisis are (1) the family covenants, the commitments and rules that are implicitly or explicitly evident; (2) the family calling, the goals and values for the adolescent and the family; and (3) the family's centeredness,

Figure 6. The identity triangle.

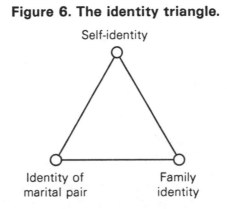

the degree to which the family is focused on and centered in its religious traditions and values. As these three overlap the identity triangle as seen in Figure 7, balance in the various components and maintaining an optimum level of tension between them are paramount. The two additional issues represented by the double lines connecting each of the points are communication and conflict management. Each of these will be examined in detail.

Family Identity. Healthy families which exist intact for a number of years develop a strong identity. If over a number of generations they maintain a residence in a general locality, that identity will be communicated in society. However, nomadic families have little or no identity in their new social communities and receive little reinforcement or resources from the community. For example, the Rowatt family, having lived three generations in a small southern Illinois mining town, has an identity in that community tied to the vocation and family lifestyle of all three generations. However, when my wife and I and our preschool twins lived in an apartment in Dallas, Texas, for three months while consulting with Park City Baptist Church, we had little or no family identity in the new community. People did not know what we valued or who we were before we left for another community. There was very limited interaction with the community and almost no support, except for a few persons also involved in the consultation.

Figure 7. Identity triangle overlapped by three dynamics.

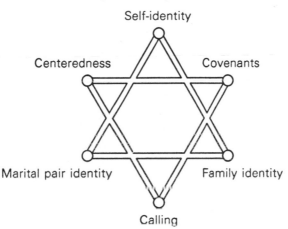

Self-identity

Centeredness   Covenants

Marital pair identity   Family identity

Calling

When one child was hospitalized in Dallas, the crisis rested on our shoulders with little support from the community. However, when a member of the family was hospitalized in our small Illinois mining town, there was a multitude of flowers cards, phone calls, and personal visits from community members with long-lasting relationships—a much greater support system. The family identity is a significant factor in pastoral care and counseling with adolescents in crisis. It can be a major support, or it may be a burden for some who want to escape its impact.

Marital Pair Identity. The identity of the marital pair, like that of the family, has a community and a cultural dimension . Nevertheless, for the crisis' sake, the most significant component of the marital pair's identity is how it is viewed by the adolescent. If the marital pair is perceived as a mutually committed, highly competent functioning team, the adolescent will consider them as a resource in time of crisis. This positive image may be based on the adolescent's lack of awareness of the couple's problems, especially when the couple is not open, but usually tension is difficult to camouflage. Adolescents can quickly determine that their parents are getting along and respond with trust and hope. When the parents function collaboratively, the adolescent can face crises more confidently.

A second perception of the marital pair is as opponents. When adolescents view their parents as opponents, they will frequently form temporary coalitions with one parent or the other and try to play the resulting power struggle for private gain. Not only will this add to the crisis dimension of an adolescent's life, it will slow the maturation and self-identity process. Furthermore, when external crises arise, the adolescent will be less confident in turning to either parent for support. The parents' inability to collaborate will decrease their power as a resource.

A third identity model is the functional-dysfunctional model. When the adolescent perceives one parent to be functional and the other dysfunctional, the adolescent will usually collaborate with one parent and will correspondingly develop either a functional or dysfunctional concept. If an adolescent collaborates with the perceived functional parent, there is the danger of enmeshing identities in that relationship, causing potential marital difficulties and limiting the adolescent's own identity formation. This develops the risk of emotional or physical incest. If on the other hand the identification is with the perceived dysfunctional parent, the adolescent will probably model parallel dysfunctional behavior that will precipitate a number of crises. In an alcoholic family, for example, an adolescent who identifies with the substance-abuse parent is also likely to turn to substance abuse as a way of acting out and avoiding stress.[2] This move not only limits the adolescent's individual identity formation but also adds to the stressors evident in a crisis.

When the adolescent sees both parents as dysfunctional, the result is confusion and disarray. With little positive role modeling, the adolescent almost invariably takes on a dysfunctional identity unless, through other social institutions (school, church, or government agency), the child receives unusual nurture and discipline for movement toward adulthood. Dysfunctional-dysfunctional situations merit strong consideration for out-of-home placement in times of crisis. When out-of-home placement facilities are poor or nonexistent, some churches provide alternative living contexts for adolescents with two dysfunctional parents.

When a parent has divorced and remarried or is living with a lover, adolescents are less likely to perceive the parental dyad as functional, especially if the stepparent's age is close to that of the adolescent. When adolescents are brought into blended families, extended family counseling is highly recommended. More than a few blended family parents find that crises erupt when their children reach puberty.

Self-identity. While Ackerman primarily addressed the self-identity of the parents, self-identity in our context is from the perspective of the adolescent. The adolescent's self-identity is reinforced primarily from family role and functioning; however, secondary reinforcement comes from personal achievements and the youngster's relationship to school, to special activities and hobbies, to the church, and to the peer group. Adolescents who have a job begin some identity formation around the kind of work they do. The self-identity of adolescents is also tied to their body image and to their acceptance of their sexuality. If they are uncomfortable with their maleness or femaleness, their identity will be correspondingly confused. Not only does the lack of positive self-identity appear as a developmental crisis, it can add to the likelihood of an adolescent's acting out behaviorally and precipitating an emergency crisis. Young people who are diagnosed as emotionally disturbed, depressed, or having conduct disorders show more self-image disturbances than normal adolescents. Emotionally disturbed adolescents show not only self-image deficiencies but also patterns of deficiencies correlated with the type of disturbance.[3]

From a theological point of view, self-image can be reinforced for adolescents from the doctrines of creation, incarnation, and redemption. Adolescents who believe they are created in the image of God, that God enters into the form of a person, even an adolescent person, and that God so loved the world (including the adolescent world) that he gave his only-begotten Son that whosoever believeth should not perish but have everlasting life, will find a foundation for a positive sense of self.

Adolescents need to be able ultimately to affirm "I am a person of worth in the image of God (male and female)" to live abundantly and to love and serve committedly (see *Being Me* by Grady Nutt). Disturbance in the family (divorce, death, prolonged illness, or unemployment) negatively affects personality development.[4] Religious faith supports positive personality development even during family crises.

One study of adolescence prepared at Catholic University showed that the most positive subgroup for self-image was black adolescents,[5] and a 1987 Gallup youth survey revealed that black teens attend church more often.[6] Ninety-three percent of black teens and 85 percent of white teens markedly agree or mostly agree on the response "I take a positive attitude toward myself"; 68 percent of black and 49 percent of white teens had attended worship in the past week.

In discussing this finding with a number of black men (pastors, athletes, and businessmen), I discovered they were not surprised. They felt that black teens receive negative press and are largely misunderstood by most white professionals. They pointed to the strong role of religion in black history and the high esteem given in the black church to the pastor. One former NFL player said that black ministers are role models for black males just as sports heroes are, but more available and accessible.

A black youth in a support group at the hospital refused to talk about his feelings for his mother and offered "I'm tough and mean" language to defend himself against peer pressure to share. After the group he handed me a touching note of explanation. This unchurched youth lacked the ego strength to share his love for his mother, but the feelings were present and could be shared with a religious leader.

Covenants

As stated earlier, Ephesians 5:21 places a covenant at the center of family relationships. Mutual, voluntary commitment is espoused by the writer of Ephesians. "Be subject to one another" demands that parents and children, like husbands and wives, enter a covenant of 100 percent commitment. This is not based on one another's desirability or worth but on reverence for the relationship to the Christ. A covenant is a promise based on the nature of the covenant maker, not on the conditions of the relationship or the nature of the recipient. The covenant is communicated first to the child through the parents' keeping of covenants in marriage. By the time the child reaches adolescence, she or he is capable of making a mutual covenant with the parents. Such covenants and contracts call for mutual respect and for negotiation of the rules, regulations, and expectations of both the parents and the adolescent (Eph. 6:1–4). Adolescents who live in a covenant relationship with their parents experience fewer crises and are more capable of managing the crises that do arise.

Calling

Matthew 16:25 paradoxically states, "For whoever would save his life will lose it, and whoever loses his life for my sake will find it." A sense of calling may inform the family and the marital pair's identity long before the child is able to conceptualize vocation. But for adolescents, a sense of calling is a way of conceptualizing vocation, an informed perception of their sense of giftedness, their resources, and talents. They find a sense of self by asking how those gifts can be dedicated to service to God and to the betterment of society. A sense of calling asks them to use their resources sacrificially to serve humanity. Adolescents who have a sense of motivation to help society or to serve their country or to seek a profession are more highly motivated and less likely to be in crisis. Those who lose themselves in their sense of calling find themselves from the sense of identity formation.

Centeredness

Centeredness is the degree to which one's identity personally is rooted in one's relationship to the Power beyond one's self. However this relationship is described, be it in "Higher Power" language of the Twelve Steps of Alcoholic Anonymous, in the traditional Christian language of piety centered in Christ, or in terms of transpersonal psychology's understanding of being centered within self, the dynamic is the same for adolescents. The center of meaning provides values for their experience of change and crisis. From their centeredness they develop a positive sense of self-identity. The content of faith experiences and the stage of religious experience as defined by James Fowler are closely interrelated in their affect on self-identity formation.[7] Stage alone does not determine identity.

Family Stressors

A number of dynamics figure prominently in the role of family stressors in adolescent crises. We will discuss internal factors and external factors. Basic to any form of crisis management is good communication.

Effective communication and the ability to have a functioning, open, and mutual conflict-resolution process depend on the degree of cohesion between the self-identity, pair identity, and family identity and the interrelatedness of covenant, calling, and centeredness.

Effective communication between parents and among family members is crucial during the adolescent period. Good communicators speak clearly and openly about a variety of topics, share not only thoughts but also feelings, and are in touch with verbal and nonverbal signals. Capable families employ a problem-solving method that openly invites input from all family members and is egalitarian, not authoritarian, in nature. Strong families set limits and maintain some executive function in the parents. Parents who lack the capacity to set caring, firm limits add to the anxiety and confusion of their adolescents in crisis. As the adolescent matures, participation in conflict management can increase in the decision-making stage of selecting the alternatives to be pursued, as discussed in chapter 4. Ultimately, as the adolescent assumes a differentiated self-identity, she or he assumes personal responsibility for decision-making and the parents move into a consultative, supportive, collaborative way of relating.

Internal Factors

The adolescent's family appears as an ever-changing, somewhat confusing, and often fear-filled unit that brings some crises upon itself. These crises erupt from internal conditions of the family system.

Major internal stressors on the adolescent's family are the struggle for dependence vs. independence, the maintenance of distance vs. closeness, and the planning of family time around the dysfunctional vs. the functional parent. External stressors have to do with illness or death of a family member, divorce, the disintegration of the marital pair, and defining family roles and expectations.

In interviewing a number of adolescents, **dependence vs. independence** surfaced in one way or another as a major concern. They said things like "Our parents need to understand that we have a mind of our own. They can't choose our friends. We can think for ourselves." On the other hand, in interviewing parents, the other side of the dependence/independence struggle was a frequent complaint. Parents would lament, "They are associating with a crowd that's not good for them. They talk back! They don't want to spend any time with the family. They're trying to act too old for their own good."

In reviewing cases of adolescents admitted to a psychiatric inpatient facility, I discovered that all but a few mentioned family dependence/independence issues as a part of the crisis. Family problems and family stress, while not necessarily the precipitating factor in the hospitalization, surfaced as a dynamic along with other factors. In a multidimensional assessment process, family dynamics almost always need separate, focused attention. Therefore, family-oriented pastoral counseling is a necessary resource that churches need to provide. Because of the demanding nature of a pastor's responsibilities, few pastors can afford the time for in-depth family counseling. Counseling centers or special church staff members are needed to fill the gap and to assist families in appropriately blessing their teenagers' movement toward independence.

The struggle between parents and adolescents for **distance vs. intimacy** should not be confused with dependency. Youngsters who spend very little time with their parents can still be dependent on their parents for their identity while those who spend a great deal of time around their parents might be quite independent from their parents in their thinking, feeling, and functioning. Distance and closeness focus not so much on time together as on the ability to share affirmation, develop emotional intimacy, and discuss ideas and plans. Close families have regular, planned, structured activities and time together. And when a crisis comes, the communication and decision-making skills developed in that regular time together undergird managing the crisis. The closeness provides a caring context for crisis resolution. As a fifteen-year-old victim of sexual molestation put it, "I knew my parents would always be there for me no matter what happened."

Distance is particularly difficult in the modern American Anglo family because of the pursuit of economic advancement. Fathers are frequently uninvolved at home and, unless special attention is given to the dynamics of managing a two-career marriage, mothers often are less available than mothers of previous decades who did not go out to work. Children who have limited bondedness with parents are prime candidates to become crisis-laden adolescents.[8]

Distance can arise from a lack of emotional bonding caused by extended periods of illness, substance abuse, or times of separation (as in prison or the military). Some children miss forming a bond early and suffer tremendously in adolescence.

Dysfunctional parenting refers to parents who have not

sufficiently formed their own self-identity and who themselves participate in deviant antisocial behavior. For example, alcoholics, drug addicts, and those institutionalized for an extended period of time in a mental hospital or prison may be dysfunctional parents. Family stress caused by the dysfunctional parent distresses not only the relationship but also the structure of the family. An adolescent who grows up with an inadequate family structure lacks the context for developing a positive self-identity. In my estimation over 50 percent of patients in psychiatric institutions have dysfunctional parents. Patients who lack a family structure have the poorest prognosis for recovery. Of the several internal factors producing stress on the family, having a dysfunctional parent creates more lasting negative effects on adolescents than any other factor.

External Factors

External stressors on the family, such as the extended illness of one parent, produce a time of crisis for the adolescent. While these factors usually can't be prevented, they can be helped.

In **serious illness** the structure, style of parenting, and general family rules and expectations are frequently thrown into disarray because the family's energy and concern are focused on the hospitalized parent. If the parent is critically ill or injured, it may be the first time the adolescent considers the possibility of a parent's mortality. Adolescents may fill the vacuum created by the attention of the family on the ill member by declaring more independence for themselves. The stress from the illness may generate enough anxiety that youngsters begin to act out and experiment sexually. Substance abuse is a common way of "managing" the pressure. If teens can turn to positive resources—other family members, caring adults, a church group or professional friend—they are better able to manage the stress and not create further crises for themselves and their families.

The **death or suicide** of a family member is a time of grief so overwhelming that unless the adolescent is given regular, almost daily attention, acting out at an unacceptable level is to be expected. One adolescent whose mother took her own life when he was fourteen wanted to leave home forever. However, after spending a week of almost round-the-clock time with the pastor, he returned to a positive relationship with his remaining parent. Rather than go to an out-of-state boarding school, he attended a private school nearby and lived at home with his father.

Divorce, the death of the parents' marriage, is another traumatic experience. With careful crisis management, the adolescent can successfully respond and even grow. However, several dynamics need consideration. Frequently, teenagers will blame themselves and the stress they have placed on the family for causing the divorce. Such borrowed guilt is unrealistic and may help force the adolescent further into crisis. In the confusion of a divorce, adolescents frequently have inadequate information about their parents' plans. Pastoral care needs to focus on encouraging teenagers and their parents to speak openly about the future, including the parents' intentions as to marriage, living arrangements, financial arrangements, and so forth. When divorce means moving, with a resulting disruption of the peer group, this is a major concern for adolescents. Not infrequently, they will manipulate and play games in an attempt to get their parents back together. (This effort only adds to the crisis, in most cases.) Joining support groups with other teens and talking with those whose parents have already divorced has helped many.

Defining roles is a further external stressor for adolescents. In families where the male or female role is closed to redefinition, adolescents who do not follow their parents' choice of roles have additional conflict. For example, a housewife who finds her role quite fulfilling might experience conflict with a teenage daughter who chooses to pursue a profession and rebels against an assigned role as homemaker. Likewise, a son who disdains athletics may feel parental pressure as he seeks a career in music. A minister's support for the freedom to be oneself helps teens cope with role pressure. Ministers can help reduce the stress by interpreting the role conflict with the parents.

Care and Counseling Resources for the Family

The first task for pastoral care and counseling with families and adolescents in crisis is to establish rapport while **assessing the dynamics** of the crisis. Ministers can and should be involved in family counseling, because we see the family cycle from birth to death and have an ongoing defined relationship with families. It is easier for the minister who already relates well to the family to intervene in an ensuing crisis in a positive way. However, caution should be taken not to presume upon the relationship and to contract openly for any crisis counseling. Because ministers sometimes lack adequate training or sufficient time or may overidentify with the family, long-term crisis counseling may need to be referred.

Assuming the minister continues in the crisis intervention at some level, the task of assessment can be facilitated by the family dynamic model introduced earlier in this chapter (see Figure 7). The minister's first task in assessment is to look at the identity triad to ascertain the identity formation level and faith development of the adolescent, the family, and the marital pair. Focus not only on the strength of each of these but also on the clarity of boundaries between them. The minister needs to be particularly alert for confusion of boundaries between the adolescent and the marital pair; parents occasionally emotionally, if not physically, use an adolescent as a mate substitute when the marriage lacks substance.

Furthermore, the minister needs to assess the level of commitment and the clarity and reciprocity of the nature of the covenants between the adolescent and the parents. Next, assessment turns to a sense of understanding of calling or mission for the family as a whole and for the adolescent in particular. Calling greatly affects the adolescent's involvement in academic pursuits and clarifies his or her identity. Finally, the minister will want to assess the adolescent's centeredness or groundedness in a meaningful personalized faith system. What does the adolescent believe? How does this affect the way the adolescent is relating to the crisis? The shepherding mode of sustaining as presented in chapter 1 is a key perspective during the assessment process. Some persons become impatient when help isn't immediately forthcoming.

A significant part of pastoral care and counseling involves assisting the family and the adolescent in **developing some simple communication rules**, such as respectfully listening to one another until each person has finished talking, checking out assumptions before acting, and interpreting nonverbal signals without clarification. The minister will also want to aid the family in expanding its communication to deeper levels so that members can send and receive clear signals about their thoughts, beliefs, and feelings. In working with communication, the shepherding mode of informing and guiding is paramount.

The shepherding perspective of healing and reconciling

blend with that of confrontation as the minister helps family members in **dealing with their methods of resolving conflicts**. While all families experience conflict, healthy families can define the conflict, mobilize their resources, and grow through creative responses. Such functioning families define their problems and mobilize resources for coping with the conflict until resolutions can be found from external resources. Families with dysfunctional relationships may or may not be able to define the problem, however, and their relationships begin to deteriorate. Isolation replaces intimacy as the conflict mushrooms. Dysfunctional families begin to disintegrate structurally as the conflict continues unresolved. Matthew 18: 15–22 provides one approach to conflict management that openly faces differences, puts reconciliation as a primary goal, and utilizes a peacemaking process for resolving the conflict. Simple negotiation skills of ventilating feelings, defining problems, and seeking alternatives, incorporated with the attitudes displayed in Matthew, will greatly enhance the family's possibilities for resolving conflicts.

Clarifying values and negotiating rules call upon the shepherding mode of guiding and confronting. The minister needs to assist both the adolescent and the parents in confronting one another's expectations and inconsistent values and then guide them in the process of establishing mutually agreed-upon expectations, rules, and foundational values. The older the teenagers, the more input would be expected from them when negotiating rules and expectations. While a number of parents remain too rigid in their rules and are unilateral in establishing expectations, too many parents err in the other direction. They do not set firm, caring limits or spend enough time in family activities for the adolescent to model the parents' values. Adolescents become anxious and overly experimental when given more freedom than they can handle.

The behavior on the adolescent unit in a psychiatric hospital improved dramatically when patients were simply placed in a routine where firm limits and clear expectations for appropriate behavior and schoolwork were set. Since each adolescent develops at his or her own pace, there is no way a given set of rules can be established for them all. The rules must be renegotiated periodically around the formula of increased freedom with increased responsible behavior and responsibility for self.

Adolescents and parents struggle to discover a unique balance of law and grace as they model the struggle of human freedom and destiny. Parents must be careful, on the one hand, not to play God with their offsprings' future. On the other hand they need to be careful not to be so distant and withdrawn as to appear unconcerned and uncaring. Some critical decisions need mutual ongoing negotiation, such as when the adolescent will seek employment, how the adolescent chooses friends and what family resources are available to entertain those friends, and what are to be the adolescent's continued dating relationships and vocational decisions.

In a crisis, the family may need assistance in reassessing these issues in light of the crisis issues. "What effect does this crisis have upon the young person's development?" is a key question for the family to resolve.

A pastoral response calls for the minister to be involved and available to the family but for the family members ultimately to make their own decisions as to the structure, relationship patterns, intimacy levels, and identity formation that are uniquely theirs. A minister may be helpful in clarifying alternatives for out-of-home placement or boarding schools if the family structure needs to be redefined. Certainly a minister needs to be of assistance in clarifying the nature of Christian relationships and parent-child relationships. There will be many disappointments for both adolescents and their parents. As the shepherd facilitates reconciliation through confession and forgiveness, the family unit can be maintained. However, in families that insist upon scorekeeping and projecting blame, a lot of confrontation of both sides will be needed.

6

Sexual Problems

God created sex and didn't say "Oops!" but pronounced sex and the rest of creation as good. In Genesis the purpose of sex is seen as procreation and relational intimacy. Sex belongs in the church; it should not be the province of smut peddlers and pornography dealers. Healthy Christian attitudes toward sex, like those expressed in David Mace's book *The Christian Response to the Sexual Revolution* and William Cole's *Sex and Love in the Bible,* are important for ministers who hope to help adolescents with crises related to sex.[1] Nevertheless, the adolescent's attitudes and values will be the foundation for his or her behavior and actions. The adolescent cannot borrow the minister's values.

Sexual problems do not begin in adolescence. They begin at an early age, when correct sex information, attitudes, and behaviors are not taught in the home. Teenagers who have received accurate information from Mom and Dad and can talk freely about values and sexual relationships are less likely to be in difficulty. However, concentrating on the past is seldom of much help at the onset of a crisis. Soon those helping the adolescent must turn to questions about the future. As John W. Whitehead, a Virginia attorney, says about talking with boys and girls about teenage pregnancy, "I think it is more important to decide where to go from there than to dwell on what has already been done. The teen faces several alternatives, and it is important that parents provide guidance to help their child select the best one."[2]

Adolescents in talk-back sessions in various churches around America have listed sex as the number one crisis they face. Adults list alcohol and drugs as the major crisis; even so, 47 percent of the ministers I surveyed who work with adolescents said that sexual problems were a high or urgent need in their church. While 26 percent felt their church did a good or an excellent job in providing sex counseling, 27 percent said their church's ministry to youth with sexual problems was poor or nonexistent. Unique pastoral issues confront ministers who are counseling with teens who face sex crises. While an inadequate foundation in sex education may have contributed to the adolescent's problem, sex education and discussions of values are only the beginning point for responding to the crisis.

Adolescent Pregnancies

Pregnancy is a major crisis from a variety of perspectives. Adolescent girls are considered high-risk obstetrical patients. Pregnant teenagers often do not complete their education. The pregnancy of an adolescent daughter is a major trauma from the family's perspective. Adolescent pregnancies produce problems for the community, economically, in that these young mothers are ill prepared for the labor force. They have special needs for the care of their infants, and they are more than likely to be lifelong welfare clients. Likewise, churches and the theological community face a crisis. They often see adolescent pregnancy as a moral issue and inadequately meet the faith needs of young pregnant women.

The sheer magnitude of the problem for Americans can be overwhelming. The United States has an adolescent pregnancy rate that is over 50 percent higher than any other industrial country in the West. The rate of adolescent pregnancy in the United States for 15- through 19-year-olds is 96 per 1,000, compared to 14 per 1,000 in countries like the Netherlands.[3] The American high pregnancy rate is attributed to a lack of adequate sex education, a lack of adequate access to confidential contraceptive services, and confused messages about sex, including a bombardment from the media. A review of 2,293 adolescents who participated in a teenage pregnancy program sponsored by the Louisville and Jefferson County Board of Education and the Department of Obstetrics at the University of Louisville School of Medicine showed that medical problems could be overcome but concluded that "the social and psychological consequences are not so readily corrected."[4] Only a few American cities of over 100,000 have developed programs to meet the needs of pregnant adolescent girls. While these programs are not always comprehensive in their coverage of nutritional information, sex education, parenting education, and counseling, these programs can still significantly modify the adverse medical results and can positively influence the offspring of these patients.

A University of Pennsylvania study paints a gloomy picture for the children of unmarried teenagers: "The offspring of teenage childbearers are doing substantially worse academically, emotionally, and socially than the children of women who had their first child after age 20." Over half the children, most of whom were in their late teens at the time of the follow-up, had repeated a grade in school, and nearly half had been suspended or expelled from school within the last five years. A large proportion admitted they regularly used drugs or alcohol, and 16 percent had attempted to run away from home.[5] While special attention needs to be given to teenage mothers and fathers, extreme long-term follow-up care must also be given to their offspring if crises are to be reduced for future generations of youth.

Few churches address the need of adolescent pregnancies except to deliver strong moral admonitions against them. The fathers frequently face many frustrations. Even those who want to have contact with their offspring or want to get married find few resources outside their own family to assist them.

Several issues are critical for counseling unmarried pregnant adolescents. Ministers tend to focus first on the guilt issue. A counselor should not project guilt from a personal value system onto an adolescent. Some girls view their pregnancy as a badge of honor and do not begin counseling by discussing guilt. Others begin with anger as the key issue. Questions about self and identity formation are perhaps the most significant long-range issues. A pregnancy may be an attempt to foreclose on an identity or to forfeit self-differentiation from the family by fulfilling the family's wish to bring a child back into the system. I have seen cases where it was as if the pregnancy was to give the teenager's parents a baby. In many cases the baby becomes a hostage of either the adolescent mother, who needs a plaything to love, or the grandparents, who are attempting to meet unmet marital needs.

Furthermore, the minister dealing with adolescent pregnancies needs to address several pragmatic issues immediately. Does the teenager have a comfortable place to live? Is there a need for reconciliation and healing with her family? Does she have medical, legal, and financial care? What provisions are made for her education?

While some pastoral counselors will choose to address alternatives such as abortion or adoption, these may not be the key long-term issues for the adolescent. While pro-life groups would rejoice with the statement of John Whitehead that the first step is to discuss the Bible teachings about the sanctity of human life and to help the teens consider that abortion is not at all an alternative, others say that addressing such an authoritarian statement to the adolescent has very little impact. Preaching at them in general has been less effective than sitting down with them and seeking to understand their value system. They should be encouraged to look at their situation in light of their knowledge of the scripture and their personal understanding of theology. At that point they can begin to make their own decisions. Sixty percent of pregnant teenage girls go ahead and give birth out of wedlock, and 96 percent of these young mothers keep their babies.[6]

Many pastoral counselors will be in touch with services for adoption and with resources such as school clinic programs or special high schools for pregnant girls like the Teen-Age Parent Program (TAPP) in Louisville, Kentucky. However, unless ministers have worked regularly with the community on such issues, they will need to first acquaint themselves with the available resources for abortion information, adoption services, marriage, keeping the child, or the parents raising the child. Adolescents are usually unskilled and need help in learning to care for an infant.

When a plan has been established, many significant issues still remain. The adolescent girl may have to deal with grief over the loss of the relationship to the father of her child, over the loss of the child itself, or with the change of her self-image. David Rolfe, Program Supervisor for Family Life Education at the Luther Social Services of Washington, in Spokane, states that among 14- to 18-year-olds who plan to get married following premarital pregnancy, he found an unusually high number who had lost a significant person through death within the preceding two years. He states, "In almost every couple out of over a hundred interviewed, one or both persons had suffered this type of loss." He points out that, in a separate study of couples receiving counseling, out of 42 women who had been pregnant premaritally, 34 had lost fathers through death or separation.[7]

Developmental issues are often not discussed: how the pregnancy affects formation of self, the differentiation from parents, the plans for education and vocational development, relationship to peers, understanding of God, and the development of one's faith. Furthermore, the issues of future sexual activities and developing a mature attitude about one's body are vital. Since a large number of adolescents deliver by cesarean section, the impact of the scar should not be overlooked. That, like a pregnant body image, can have a more traumatic effect on the psyche of the adolescent girl than discovering she was pregnant in the first place.

A seventeen-year follow-up study of pregnant adolescents found that three factors most critical in successfully adjusting to life after having delivered a child as a teenager were continuing with education, being able to limit births of subsequent children, and achieving a stable marriage at a later point in life.[8] Perhaps the crucial initial factors are parental support and being accepted in a community of faith.

A single mother who had given birth to her son at age 18 told me several years later that she had just won the outstanding chemistry student award in her senior college graduating class. She is preparing to enter graduate school. Her parents provided an apartment attached to their home and offered spiritual, emotional, and financial assistance for her. They have maintained a positive relationship with their grandchild. He is "at home" in their local congregation. When this young woman spoke to my pastoral counseling class in 1987, she underscored that forgiveness, not judgmental condemnation and anger, is needed by churches before they can begin to minister to adolescents like herself.

Sexual Abuse

Rape and sexual abuse (homosexual and heterosexual) traumatize children and adolescents. While statistics are difficult to compile, most specialists agree that reported cases of sexual abuse of children and adolescents have increased dramatically in the past decade.

The incidence of sexual abuse inside and outside the family is much higher for females.[9] Stepfamilies are probably even more vulnerable to the stresses from abuse, since their boundaries are less clear. Incestuous impulses between adolescents and opposite-sex parents are more likely to increase, particularly in conflicted families. A previously special and loving relationship between a daughter and a father could evolve into a mutually hostile one as a way of protecting the daughter from becoming provocative or the father from becoming posses- sive.

Like pregnancy, sexual abuse has a major impact on the development of self-identity as well as on a young person's relationship to the parents. Children and adolescents abused by someone other than a parent or stepparent will often dis- tance themselves from their parents and wonder why they weren't better protected. One youngster told of trying to re- fuse to go to a particular house where she was being abused. Her mother forced her to go and never seemed to suspect that abuse was the issue. Parents who themselves are deal- ing with unresolved mid-life sexual issues will have added con- flicts with their adolescents and are especially ill prepared to deal with issues of abuse and teenage sexual identity.

In dealing with sexual abuse, it is important to hear the entire story, deal with accurate information, and support legal as well as social intervention on behalf of the adolescent. In fact, it is a violation of law not to report the physical and sexual abuse of a minor.

Some teens are reluctant to report sexual abuse for fear of losing their family if they seek help. Fear of repercussions from the perpetrator can also delay reporting. A sense of shame and doubt stops others. Intense anger, often having no real direc- tion or focus, can lead to violence or be internalized in dark depression. A few teens escape into fantasy and hallucinations to avoid the reality of the abuse. One girl said, "I learned to pretend I was someone else when my stepfather would force himself upon me. Now that it's all stopped, I don't know who I really am."

Secondary complications, such as failure in school, rebel- lious conduct, shyness, and hallucinations are often the precipitating events that initiated counseling. It seems particu- larly true that adolescents who have lost the capacity to be critical of their parents are often victims of abuse (emotional, physical, or sexual).

When counseling abused teenagers reaffirm their worth as persons through the doctrines of creation, incarnation, and redemption. Deal openly with any fears and transference is- sues before long-term counseling is contracted for. Usually it is best for female counselors to see girls and male counselors to see boys, but this is not always the case. There is some evidence that abuse affects one's concept of God as well as the view of one's own parents. Reconciliation and forgiveness usually come in the latter period of dealing with sexual abuse issues. However, sustaining begins with the first hint of abuse and continues undiminished.

While abuse is usually a family issue, this is not the case for rape. Homosexual and heterosexual rapes of adolescents are on the increase as adolescents move more quickly into society and away from the protection of their parents and as sexual gratification becomes a more highly valued goal of life. The use of sex in advertising contributes to underlying attitudes that cheapen not only our view of sex but our view of what it means to be a person. Rape victims need special attention (available in many community rape relief centers) and ongoing peer support groups. While the minister will want to continue to support the person, referral and professional help seem wisest, unless the minister has specialized counseling certification. The family, parents as well as siblings of the victim, also needs care and attention. Many times the minister can counsel the family after the victim has been referred.

Sexual Promiscuity

The level of sexual promiscuity among adolescents varies from culture to culture. However, most experts agree that parents are unaware of the extent of adolescent sexual activity. Many ministers also do not realize how widespread it is. One middle-school counselor found that 60 percent of the sixth-, seventh-, and eighth-graders in her school reported having intercourse at least once and a large number were involved in oral sex. Other studies say that from 70 to 80 percent of high school seniors report having had sexual intercourse and a significant number, perhaps 30 to 50 percent, are sexually active and promiscuous. As one adolescent said in protest to her counselor's suggestion that she date several boys in order to find out what kind of person she liked, "You're in the dark ages. Nobody dates around, because if you are dating somebody, you are having sex, and if you are dating around, you are having sex with a lot of people. I don't want to be seen as that kind of girl."

It seems that few adolescents reduce their level of sexual activity. Once they become sexually active, few ever stop. Therefore education before they start is essential. The lack of adequate sex education is likely to contribute to promiscuity. Many teens experiment with sex "to see what it's like." Training in the home and the attitudes and values of parents seem to be the most potent factor in postponing sexual activity among adolescents. Parents who are open to discussion, provide accurate information, and model a healthy theology of sex encourage their adolescents to postpone sexual activity. Excitement, curiosity, and ignorance are key factors in initiating sexual experimentation. Parents who are close to their children and meet their intimacy needs without overcontrol are at less risk of having promiscuous adolescents.

Pastoral counselors who work with promiscuous adolescents will also have to deal with their parents' feelings. These may range from anger, guilt, and grief to indifference, amusement, or pride. However, assisting adolescents to make personal decisions about their sexual activity and adequate birth-control methods comes early on the counseling agenda.

Understanding the adolescent's own value system and personality struggle paves the way for showing how to use that value system in a rational, integrated way in making decisions about future sexual activity. As one sixteen-year-old said, "When I have to worry about birth control, it makes me think about the kind of girl I have become, and I don't want to be that kind of girl, so I am going to stop having intercourse—until I'm old enough to handle it." When the decisions are internalized by adolescents, they are more likely to influence their lifestyle and behavior.

Alcohol and drugs are closely related to promiscuity. Parties where social pressure and substance abuse break down impulse control and resistances are notorious for their sexual activity. One fifteen-year-old girl's response to the suggestion that she require her lover to use a condom was, "Hell, I'm so drunk most of the time I don't know who he is, let alone whether or not he's wearing a condom. You don't understand the kind of parties I go to." The multidimensional nature of adolescent crises is demonstrated most dramatically in these areas.

Obviously, self-respect and identity formation issues are key in assisting adolescents who are promiscuous. A lack of childhood bonding and teenage blessings from parents sets the stage for sexual problems. Furthermore, a sense of brokenness in their relationship with their parents, perhaps because of their parents' divorce, can cause a general feeling of distance and loneliness that leads to a sexual search for intimacy. Some feel their parents are unconcerned. One eighteen-year-old said, "My parents don't give a damn anyway."

Adolescents need to understand the dangers of their promiscuous behavior in terms of disease, of being raped or being forced into prostitution or pornography. Many ministers are so isolated from street life they have little impact in shaping decisions and behavior of promiscuous adolescents. A few clergy who do get involved at the street level tell of many frustrations but have made some dramatic interventions. Unless we are willing to get involved, sacrifice some of our office comforts, and let go of our stereotypes, we will continue to have minimal impact. Educational materials such as those available from the National Center for Missing and Exploited Children in Washington, D.C., offer effective church and community programs.

While many teenagers have had some sexual experience, most are not sexually promiscuous. Derek Miller points out that the majority are not constantly moving from bed to bed as commonly fantasized by some adults. Promiscuity is more a symptom of disturbed, immature adolescents. He goes on to hypothesize that middle adolescents who are unsure of their own identity and have poor impulse control are particularly vulnerable to sexual promiscuity at parties. Too much freedom given to adolescents before they are mature enough to make judgments about sexuality creates a context in which promiscuity will grow. Miller concludes that promiscuous adolescent girls are not usually treatable by outpatient counseling.[10] Assisting adolescents in firming up their identity and in clarifying the structures, relationships, and limits in their family will give them the strength to make decisions about more responsible sexual behavior. Knowing and understanding what the scriptures teach about sex sets a foundation for counseling teens and their families.

Sexually Transmitted Diseases

Sexually transmitted diseases (STDs), particularly herpes and AIDS (Acquired Immune Deficiency Syndrome), have created a scare among some adolescents. It remains to be seen if patterns of sexual activity will change. Early indications are that more mature teenagers will change their behavior. The behavior of more immature teenagers will probably remain unchanged by information about AIDS and other sexually transmitted diseases. After viewing a very frank AIDS film, one group of emotionally troubled adolescents concluded that, although it was frightening, they would not behave differently.

Only one in the group said that she would change her sexual activity. The others trusted magical thinking, typified by the statement of one boy who said, "Sex is so much fun, it can't be all bad. I'm just sure I won't get AIDS."

The widespread sexual involvement among adolescents has led Judith Mishne to quote a New York Society for Adolescent Psychiatry newsletter that sex has become "like McDonald's hamburgers"—that is, it is easy to get, cheap, and essentially tasteless. Mishne urges that "infections spread by sexual contact must be understood by adolescents and by all persons engaged in professional work with teenagers because sexually transmitted diseases are running rampant in America."[11] However, all sexually transmitted diseases are not transmitted by sexual intercourse. Many can be spread by oral sex and some by passionate kissing. The common emotional reaction of adolescents who learn that they have herpes or another nonlethal sexual disease is still shock and a frantic search for a cure. They develop a sense of loneliness and isolation. Upon reflection, anger and fear about the future may set in. It is not uncommon for a "leper" effect to appear and precipitate deep depression and perhaps underlying pathology.[12]

AIDS has moved into the heterosexual as well as gay community. No one has yet been known to recover. Because the disease can lie latent for three to ten years, thousands of people can be infected unknowingly. Therefore, an adequate AIDS education program that informs adolescents how AIDS is transmitted—that is, through body fluids, usually by sexual contact or sharing a needle—and how AIDS is *not* transmitted—one does not become infected through casual social contact—can help. Some groups have predicted that the use of prophylactics or condoms is about 90 percent effective in preventing AIDS. But even then there is a realistic chance of spreading the disease. While depression and disturbance set in for persons with all incurable diseases, the needs of AIDS patients go beyond that level. Because of their profound loneliness and social isolation, AIDS patients need specialized treatment centers and ongoing care. The minister or pastoral counselor needs to be very sensitive to the family and, whenever possible, facilitate open communication and a growing relationship with the AIDS patient. Even planning the funeral requires special sensitivity and attention. It is not uncommon for AIDS patients to be suicidal. Unless a minister has specific training, a referral must be a strong consideration.

Pastoral Care Responses

Several principles of care need to be underscored as we reflect on ministry with adolescents in sexual crisis. These guidelines, of course, will need to be integrated into one's own style, philosophy, and practice of care and counseling ministry.

1. Get the facts. Deal with actualities, check out stories, and avoid catastrophizing from rumors. Because of adolescents' general lack of information about sex and ministers' frequent lack of comfort in discussing sexual issues, it is important to make the extra effort to get specific details about a given situation, set of behaviors, and related medical implications. When talking with adolescents, follow up the specifics of their comments. For example, one young man in a church group said, "Sure, I'm sexually active. I have been for several years." Since he was only fourteen, I followed up in an individual session to see what he really meant. While he seemed to be referring to having had sexual intercourse since the group was discussing pregnancy, his sexual activity had only involved private masturbation. While one might be disturbed by his concurrent use of pornographic material, that's hardly the way he would get someone pregnant.

While many adolescents will say they know a lot about sex, they are less sure of themselves when it comes to actual discussions. Many myths and twisted, distorted facts masquerade as accurate information in adolescent circles. While discussing the facts, avoid detectivelike attitudes and questions. Explore sensitively and caringly the adolescents' information, relationships, and behavioral patterns. Be as wise as the serpent and as harmless as a dove.

2. Understand their philosophy of sex from the biblical perspective. While some ministers err on the side of an authoritarian legalism that alienates adolescents in crisis, others may err on the side of insecure permissiveness. Adolescents need an opportunity to discuss their views and to understand a biblical view of sexuality. As the immediate crisis issues are resolved, reflecting upon and consolidating what was learned provide an excellent opportunity for future growth. While most adolescents will rebel against lectures and sermons given in an individual context, they are open for dialogue and serious Bible study. These discussions need to be given in the context of assisting the adolescent to contract for limits and to make some covenants with parents, peers, and pastor. A prominent adolescent psychiatrist suggests that middle adolescents particularly, who are unsure of their identity and maintain poor impulse control, might take a lack of adult supervision and guidance as permission to behave impulsively. He says that "too much freedom given to adolescents before they are mature enough to make appropriate judgments becomes a license; adults are felt not to care."[13] Although late adolescents might have a more developed sense of internal, value-based, impulse control, they still need to study and think through the physical concepts of love, commitment, and long-term caring relationships. More often than not, late-adolescent girls are looking for serious relationships while late-adolescent boys still view sex recreationally. At least, the boys seem less concerned with settling down in a serious relationship. The feminist movement is lessening this difference, particularly for young women interested in a career.

3. Keep confidentiality issues paramount. The issue of confidentiality surfaces not only in relationship to discussion with the adolescent and his or her parents but also with the larger church and professional community. More often than not, adolescents' confidences are violated. While legally they may not have certain rights for confidentiality, morally they lay claim to such. Always explain to the adolescents what you need to share about them, and with whom, and seek their permission. Only when it is viewed as endangering someone should a confidence be shared without their permission. I encourage adolescents to share information with their parents and other counselors themselves, and I offer to sit with them while they do it. Most see the need and share their crises appropriately.

As a professor at the New York University School of Social Work reminds us, "Confidentiality and the right to privacy is the cornerstone of all effective therapeutic work." She strongly warns against sharing any information.[14] This is particularly true with questions about pregnancy, birth control, sexual identity, and sexual practice. Counselors who regularly violate confidentiality issues and divulge information even with the person's best interest at heart will soon find they have lost the trust of the adolescent community.

However, the minister is in the paradoxical situation of being equally responsible to the parents, particularly if the adolescent is in his or her congregation. Great care must be taken to walk a tightrope between protecting confidentiality and being responsible to one's relationship with the larger community of faith. The best method may be to support the adolescent through approaches like role plays and the willingness to be present as the adolescent discusses these issues with the parents. Many times I have gone to parents in advance to say, "I am asking your teenager to talk with you. I want to ask you to agree to certain ground rules: that you will respect your teenager, that you will listen to the whole story, and that you will work with us to find responsible alternatives to the problem." Preparing the ground in advance in this way often makes adolescent/parent conferences quite productive.

Confidentiality must be limited by the legal responsibility to report sexual abuse and child abuse to the necessary authorities and must be shared with fellow professionals. When working as part of a caring team with an adolescent, we ask the adolescent basically to trust the entire team.

4. Assess the developmental maturity level. This is the primary factor in assessment, particularly in the area of sexuality. Just as young people enter puberty over a wide variety of ages (perhaps from ten to fourteen), they learn and develop sexually throughout adolescence at different rates. Even though an early teen, twelve to thirteen years old, may be pregnant, it doesn't mean she has a developed view of sexuality or is even comfortable talking about sex. In ministering to adolescents, understanding their developmental level is crucial to planning a ministry strategy.

5. Consider sexual crises in the larger context of growth. Teens who are having difficulty sexually need to have counselors who will not stereotype them for the rest of their adolescence. The parents of young adolescents need assistance in not catastrophizing when there has been a sexual problem. Sexual problems for young adolescents are most likely the result of experimentation and ignorance. Attention should be given to helping them find a sense of forgiveness and reconciliation with their parents and an opportunity to learn from the experience. With middle adolescents, sexual problems are usually more serious, in that they reflect an attempt to define themselves and their value system and are not just experimentations. While reconciliation and forgiveness are still key issues, a more radical stance of healing the broken self needs to inform one's ministry. Middle adolescents who are sexually active are less likely than early adolescents to change their lifestyles and patterns. This perversion of self usually involves for middle adolescents an inadequate understanding of love and a refocusing on passion as a lifestyle.

For late adolescents, who are more refined in their self-identity, sexual problems most often reflect an attempt to meet their physical needs and perhaps an unrealistic attitude that they won't get in trouble. They really think, It can't happen to me. Late adolescents also need to deal with forgiveness and reconciliation issues, but not only with their parents. They need appropriate places to form attachments apart from the family. A minister can assist them in making independent plans for independent living. When pregnancy is an issue and marriage is considered, see that marriage is a chosen commitment, not just a quick solution. The late adolescent will particularly need the sustaining presence of the minister as she or he moves from the family. Sexual problems can thwart the movement toward independence and create a dependence that is intolerable for both the parents and the older adolescent.

Usually, sexual problems are the result of attempts by an adolescent to resolve either an internal or external developmental difficulty. After the sexual issues have been resolved, the developmental difficulty may still need attention and follow-up. For example, lonely adolescents may have sex to gain acceptance and friendship. It is not an act of love or even experimentation. Helping them deal with a resulting pregnancy and then dropping them misses the deeper issue. Some professionals have felt that even sexually abused teens may have personal issues beyond the sexual crisis. Miller states that "young people who are sexually attacked have often unconsciously provoked or consented to the incident."[15] While one might disagree, at first, and point out that they certainly do not want the pain that comes with the attack, one is still wise to assess the need for deeper levels of counseling after addressing the crisis issue; through loneliness, self-rejection, or alienation a youngster may be seeking attachments in dangerous ways. Nevertheless, it must be underscored that loneliness is not seduction. It is the children and adolescents who suffer. They are victims, not accomplices.

6. Confront the society. While values will vary within social class and racial structure, there is never an excuse for adults molesting and victimizing adolescents sexually. Ministers who are concerned with adolescents who have been so victimized must confront the society and community where such issues are unaddressed. It is not enough to minister to the victim. The caring minister must attack the social structures that allow this victimization to occur.

7

Peer and Academic Pressures

Education and the acquiring of life skills is a central task of adolescents. Luke 2:52 records, "And Jesus increased in wisdom and in stature, and in favor with God and man." Such cannot be said for many troubled teenagers. While they may increase in stature, they struggle and wrestle unsuccessfully with wisdom. They have difficulty relating to peer groups and adults. They frequently congregate with other teens who are having difficulties. They do not learn to love themselves or each other. Often family problems exist. They lack a demonstrated love relationship with their parents, who push them to succeed at school. They are not in favor with peers or parents and perhaps not with God.

School and friends are major factors in the identity formation process, so this chapter will focus on the critical issues surrounding peer problems and academic pressures. Appropriate peer involvement seems to be a critical factor not only in self-differentiation and social separation from the family but also in successful negotiation of the tasks of education. Social isolation is a matter of concern to adolescents that is highly relevant to subsequent pathology and school problems.[1] Because of the interrelatedness of peer involvement and the school environment, problems in these two areas receive joint focus in this chapter. The impact of schools on peer associations is a very important current topic. Its relationship to stress makes it salient, but so does its relation to many other social issues and problems.[2]

Peer Pressure

Adolescent peer pressure is complicated by such social factors as the rapid mobility of society, increased diversification of school systems, and an exaggerated emphasis on academic performance to the exclusion of vocational alternatives. An increasing number of disturbed adolescents appear so socially isolated as to have only one or two acquaintances and no close friends. It is true that no person is an island, but some young people exist in virtual isolation from the time they leave for school in the morning until they return in the afternoon. As one teen put it, "I kinda stay to myself and never say anything. That way no one messes with you. Even the teachers leave me alone." Pain from the perceived rejection increases to the level that the teenager acts out and explodes or implodes in an attempt to seek help. In any adolescent crisis, the counselor must assess peer issues as well as school performance.

While a lack of friends will seldom bring an adolescent directly into formal counseling, it is frequently a topic of informal discussions with youth ministers and pastors. Friendships were listed as the second most critical issue on the survey of local church ministers. Seventy-one percent of those responding listed it as a high or urgent need; only 4 percent listed it as low or nonexistent. The lack of a friendship network may well be a precipitating factor in such emergencies as running away, suicide, and turning to substance abuse.

In his delightful and widely read volume *The Five Cries of Youth,* Mert Strommen offers several worthwhile suggestions for creating a network of peer support for adolescents. He reports that successful church youth workers were judged as persons who could help young people get to know one another, encourage group awareness and sensitivity in everyday life, and find Christ in and through relationships with others. Furthermore, they could become involved and make young people aware of loneliness while developing a team attitude through youth activities. Trying to build a staff community in the church could serve as a model of teamwork.[3] A part of the ministry of reconciliation as discussed in chapter 2 would respond to Strommen's report that helping youth with forgiveness and acceptance of others is an important aspect of building community. Because of hurt feelings and wounded egos, unresolved anger frequently builds walls in the youth community and works against the interlacing of support.

In formal counseling with adolescents in crisis, encouraging them to set goals for making friends constitutes a first step in assisting them toward community. However, a depressed or shame-filled youth will frequently feel unworthy. As one attractive seventeen-year-old said, "If I met me at my school, I wouldn't want to be my friend; why should anyone else?" The fear of rejection and a tendency to withdraw will work against experiencing community. However, an understanding, caring relationship with a counselor that includes aspects of friendship can be the beginning point in building a network of friends. I often ask an adolescent to make a list of former friends and to look at their characteristics as a way of finding prospective friends for themselves. However, they and I realize that most friendships develop secondarily to the pursuit of a task. With shared activities, common interests, and even the struggle toward recovery, friendships begin to develop naturally. Sometimes role-playing and coaching adolescents in handling frustrating encounters with their peers can assist them in building peer relationships. Adolescents in a psychiatric unit who were able to develop friendships tended to recover more quickly than those who remained detached.

Peer rejection can be an erroneous perception on the part of adolescents. Because of their pain, distortions of relationships are frequent. Helping teens examine the evidence around peer relationships frequently leads them to see that indeed they are as well liked as anyone else. Many times adolescents exaggerate and worsen their peer problems while at the same time generalizing that everyone must feel badly toward them.

How to make friends is an important issue for shy, lonely, and rejected teenagers. As might be expected, the adolescent's relationship to his or her family is a key factor in the capacity to make friends. Authoritarian parents who view parental rights and obligations as complementary to those of the child strongly influence the composition of their adolescent's peer friendship groups, cliques, and neighborhood friends. Consistency in moderate levels of family support and control shows up in friendly and spontaneous relationships with peers.[4] Basically, open communication and problem-solving techniques in the family serve as models for adolescent relationships with their peers and provide a secure base for the exploration of friendships. Extremely authoritarian or permissive families set up their children for rebellion, and these children become prime targets for slavish conformity to a peer group[5] or even become target recruits for cults and other countercultural movements that withdraw from society in communal-type living.[6] While rehearsal, role play, and making decisions about making friends are significant, dealing with family relationships is an equally important therapeutic issue.

Scripture encourages us to love our neighbor as ourself. Those who work with adolescents might add that they are able to love their neighbors—that is, their peers—only as they feel loved by their parents and are able to affirm an emerging self. Early adolescents are particularly troubled by fears of peer rejection and become preoccupied with notes and rumors and "who said what about whom" conversations. Middle adolescents are more solid in their peer identification, less prone to overreact to rejection, and frequently experiment with a number of peer relationships. Late adolescents are more likely to settle into a harmonious relationship with their peers, particularly if the young people are welcomed guests in the family system and if the family is open to an honest exchange of ideas with them.

Peer support or lack of peer support will evidence itself around conflicts with parents or overdependency upon parents. Since one function of the peer group is to help in the transition from dependency on the parent,[7] an overdependency on the parent could well mean the lack of age-group friends. Parents may need to plan activities and encourage their teenagers to get involved in peer-related activities. Frequently, however, when it comes time for the parents to turn loose, they are resistant or passive in their support for the adolescents' involvement. One uncovers a deeper level of fear as motivation for the parents' role in the dependency. Family counseling will perhaps be needed, along with individual counseling of the teen, in order to make new friendships possible. Adolescent growth groups and therapy groups addressing issues other than peer involvements do result in excellent peer bonding and assist in building relationships.

Pastoral Care Responses to Peer Pressure

Several counseling responses, already mentioned in previous paragraphs on peer pressures, need to be discussed in more detail. Many techniques have proven successful. However, first the adolescent must see the need and be willing to take the risk to become involved with friends. One is wise to wait for the adolescent to make a statement about the need for friends or to report some sense of rejection rather than to introduce the issue as part of the therapeutic agenda.

Family Counseling

As has been mentioned, the teenager's relationship to his or her family plays an integral role in peer issues. Giving attention to family conflicts, miscommunications, and role tensions will free the adolescent for more productive peer involvement. Many times this will mean confronting parents with their role in setting up the adolescent for broken peer relationships and even considering out-of-home programs when parents are unwilling to support their offspring. This is particularly important for any adolescent who has been emotionally abused or for late adolescents whose families are burnt out by dealing with them.

Clarifying the family rules, teaching effective communication methods, discovering conflict management techniques, and discovering mutual expectations are essential points for family therapy with adolescents who are having peer problems. However, the issues will frequently involve confused roles and relationships between the teen and one parent. Marriage issues unresolved by the parents may surface. Avoid dealing with marriage issues in the presence of the adolescent. These need to be dealt with separately.

Role Play

Small groups of adolescents who are willing to work on peer relationships and social interaction can be effectively led by the minister who is willing to utilize role-play situations to teach adolescents more effective communication and relationship skills. Role-play groups expand understanding of one another's thoughts, feelings, and values. Adolescents with poor social interaction skills may be willing to take risks in the context of the role play when they are not willing to do so in an unsupervised social situation. One such group functioned very effectively in assisting shy teens to participate in appropriate peer involvements. While most of the role plays were suggested by the adolescents, some were initiated by the leader and involved biblical stories, such as the story of the prodigal and the conflict with the elder brother. This not only served a religious education purpose but assisted the young people in looking at the value issues behind their peer relationships. While role play can be used as a rehearsal technique in individual counseling, I have found it most effective when used with groups of adolescents.

Self-Formation

Developing a positive identity apart from a family identity is a key issue for adolescents, particularly those who are yielding to negative peer pressure. Focusing on the formation of the self gives adolescents the capacity to say no when peer pressures encourage them toward antisocial behavior that might lead to further complication of a crisis. The relationship between the counselor and the adolescent can be a powerful factor in identity formation. A counselor who understands transference dynamics and can avoid negative countertransferences can be quite effective in imparting ego strength to a disturbed juvenile. Owning and claiming mutuality of the friendship can empower the young person as well as focus on issues of self.

Cliques and Prejudice

Within school systems and churches, teenagers form cliques around interests. Help them understand these dynamics. Teenagers separate themselves according to varied preferences, academic ability, level of social development, neighborhoods, and activities. Strommen found on his survey of 400 young people that young church members were particularly preoccupied with building better relationships. When asked what changes they hoped for, they mentioned "better relationships" more than twice as often than any other single issue. Surprisingly, it surfaced three times as often as having a better self-concept.[8]

While adolescents in general seem to be less prejudiced than adults,[9] race and color are still likely issues. Certainly the religious community can offer a theology of acceptance when issues of prejudice and race surface. However, rejection is a subtle, private issue, and an adolescent's preoccupation is with her or his own lack of acceptance. As young people define themselves, it is important to assist them to clarify their own values and interests apart from those of a friend. According to Kathleen Stassen Berger, professor at City University of New York, as adolescents reject particular groups they reject the particular self-definition that would go with those groups.[10] Adolescents need to know why they reject a particular group (as nerds, preps, punks, headbangers, brains, or jocks) as well as why they choose a specific clique. As they get older, peer identification will be less significant in defining self and they can be expected to become more self-directed. Middle adolescents depend on peers more than early and late adolescents.

Cognitive Distortions

Assisting adolescents to "weigh the pros and cons" before making a decision or accepting a particular interpretation to a set of events is important in helping them to deal with their perceived rejection. Remember, troubled adolescents are likely to be egocentric, not only in thinking that everyone's behavior is related to themselves but in exaggerating the importance of that behavior. They think of themselves as "right" in most situations because they concentrate only on one side.

Adolescents are apt to focus on one interpretation to an event and feel personally put down. One girl surmised that because a boy walked by without looking up from his book, "he hates me now." Because of their cognitive abilities for formal and abstract thinking, adolescents can consciously reflect on a given event and look at alternative conclusions and interpretations. As they reframe and view the context of a problem differently, their feelings of isolation and rejection are likely to change. Feelings of suspicion and persecution augment their cognitive distortions.

For instance, one girl complained that a given friend was rejecting her because that friend had "talked at lunch with Lisa, and Lisa had dated her boyfriend." As we began to clarify the facts, she became aware that it was likely that her friend was not consciously betraying her, and anyway the friend did not know about her strong dislike for Lisa. Upon reflection she decided to check out an alternative interpretation and was able to maintain her friendship and not feel personally rejected.

Conflict Management

Teaching adolescents to define a problem, list the options, and negotiate a mutually caring, win-win resolution empowers them in peer relationships. Peer rejection can happen over a rather insignificant matter because young people lack the skills to negotiate differences. Their learned patterns of handling anger might be destructive. For example, they may pull away in coldness, resort to sarcasm, deliver threats, or seek to inflict pain because they are upset. In an irrational mode and from a lack of control they explode at a friend. Assisting them to understand their anger and solve problems mutually strengthens their peer relationships. An attitude of forgiveness and a personal theology of reconciliation will fortify friendships. They and their friends will at times disappoint each other, but that need not be the end of their amity.

Academic Pressure

Although poor academic performance is a major concern for their parents, the teenagers themselves mentioned a number of other concerns more frequently in their interviews: fear for their personal safety, concern for a lack of respect from teachers, and arbitrary authoritarian rules.

Few adults understand the adolescent's world at school unless they are regularly involved. Ministers and parents need to visit the school and participate in school functions. Going to open houses and finding other special times to be in school will awaken most adults to a number of new concerns and will acquaint them with the world of adolescents. Our children spend more waking time in school than in any other one place, and yet school problems receive very limited attention in many counseling approaches.

Concerned adults frequently drag their offspring into a counselor's office and begin reciting a list of academic failures. Adolescents are likely to reject blame for many of their poor grades. They speak of injustices or lost papers and offer other excuses. A central issue can be poor communication and a lack of involvement on the parents' part. When adolescents come with academic problems, first check out the family system. Ask yourself, "What role does this crisis play within the family system?" If there is tension in the parents' marriage or if there has been a recent divorce, academic problems are understandable. The parents' stress diverts their attention from school matters. Preoccupation with grief, anxieties, and anger because of their parents' problems drains young people emotionally and makes concentrating a difficult issue. Furthermore, evaluating the parents' level of involvement in their offspring's everyday study habits and performance is fertile soil for counseling. Lack of family support is a critical issue. However, in certain subcultures of American society, too much family involvement can also be a problem. For instance, in some Asian-American families, the pressure to succeed academically is so great that the adolescents suffer low self-esteem and depression out of proportion to their peers.

Poor study habits, the lack of a study place, inability to organize assignments, and failure to maintain a calendar for planning one's workload all contribute to academic problems. Having determined that the family is involved and that study habits and place are adequate, one needs next to rule out learning disabilities or being misplaced academically. Some adolescents truly cannot do the work. Programs beyond their ability create intolerable frustrations and produce despair and detachment.

However, a large number of adolescents have poor academic performance because they do not view work in school as primary. They lack motivation. With no sense of direction (no calling) and no specific vocational involvement (no commitment), but in the presence of a "pleasure first" orientation (no centeredness), a youngster is very likely to fail at school. A popular eighteen-year-old told me six months after high school graduation that in retrospect she would gladly have sacrificed being a cheerleader for better grades and the opportunity to go to a college of her choosing.

A few teenagers have academic problems because their workload outside of school is too great. Grades decline when adolescents are employed outside of school more than ten hours a week. And when all else has failed, check out test and performance anxiety,[11] panic attack due to public exposure, and too much pressure to perform.[12]

A number of adolescents interviewed for this project reported fears for their safety. This involved personal fears in traveling to and from school. One girl in Miami confessed, "I'm afraid to get off the school bus and walk home without checking to make sure there are no cars or vans. I don't want to be raped." One young man reported that he was afraid to go to the bathroom at his school because gang members who hung out in the bathroom would extort money and sexual favors. Fears for safety obviously affect academic performance, but, more importantly, they affect the adolescent's physical and emotional health. Adults and administrators involved in schools need to address such concerns as a community-wide problem. Some urban school systems have installed metal detectors, and many search for weapons at the least hint of trouble.

Frequently, adolescents might find that the teaching in the

classroom calls into question a particular segment of their religious education and training. However, it is the rare teacher who will not recognize the student's right to disagree. More often the challenge to faith is a subtle challenge to the values of the adolescent. It is particularly difficult when churches also refuse to permit adolescents the freedom to debate issues and think for themselves. Churches that are willing to discuss science and faith issues and values with their young people find that teenagers can remain faithful while pursuing an education. In general, adolescent development is nurtured when the environment can encourage intellectual exploration.[13] As Abraham sustained by faith moved toward a new land, the faith of adolescents supports them as they move toward the fertile new lands of educational exploration.

When adolescents and parents discuss authority issue problems with the school, the adolescents may define the problem as authoritarian teachers who "had stupid rules and treated you like trash when you dared to question them"; the parents will usually speak of their children's lack of respect, sarcasm, and rudeness to teachers, counselors, and principals. The authority issue is frequently two-sided. The adolescent's anger is usually fueled by a perceived lack of respect and interest on the part of the teacher. Teachers frequently fail to negotiate and listen to the pupils' problems. Their directive approach frequently sets up a juvenile to rebel or lose self-respect. Educators who can learn to negotiate appropriately and to listen respectfully find that discipline is less of a problem in the classroom. Teacher Effectiveness Training and its active listening model has done much to improve the teacher's side of this authority problem.[14]

From the student's side the authority problem frequently stems from difficulties in relationships at home and is also a parent issue. A counselor can fully expect that a similar authority problem will develop between adolescent and counselor. Some students complain that school is like being in prison. When a pupil has been branded a troublemaker and festering issues have gone unresolved for a length of time, it is important to consider the option of changing schools. Obviously that carries with it the problem of shifting peer groups and of losing the adults (if any exist) upon whom they have begun to model themselves. Miller suggests that in school systems that move between junior high and senior high at grade 9, rather than grade 8, adolescents are less prepared for the social adjustment. It is best if movement from junior high to senior high is between early adolescence and middle adolescence, at age thirteen or fourteen, not age fifteen.[15]

Many adolescents with other serious crises see dropping out of school as a solution. The pressures of school, the overwhelming inability to catch up, and peer rejection do not lead to dropping out as frequently as do involvement in gangs, drugs, or alcohol or pregnancy. The dropout is a loser and creates problems for society. School dropouts have a difficult time ever adjusting economically. Studies suggest that high school dropouts will earn several hundred thousand dollars less in their lifetime than their peers who finish high school. In states where the GED (General Education Diploma) is possible before age eighteen, that is one alternative. But dropouts have few choices. After teens have gotten more than two years behind, it is very unlikely that they will return to the classroom and complete their education. Juveniles who drop out of high school and can be geared toward vocational and job training fare better than those who do not.

Pastoral Care Responses to Academic Pressure

Obviously, understanding vocational and guidance counseling from the educational viewpoint will assist any minister. However, it is best that the minister work as a part of the team and also refer adolescents and their families to the school counselor. This frees the minister to focus his or her counseling in other areas.

Assisting adolescents to **understand their purpose in life** and the calling of God for their life adds to the motivation of academic involvement. Education prepares young people for life in general, but a particular goal motivates them to try harder at school. Teens need guidance in discovering their gifts, support in developing them, and confrontation to dedicate them in service to others.

A minister can also interpret viewpoints and **facilitate communication with the parents**. Relieving some stress and increasing the family support creates an environment where academic problems can be addressed creatively. While some parents need to lower their expectations, others need to assert a whole new sense of direction in their offspring's education. While some teens need to increase their expectation and exert more effort, others need to know how to ask their parents for help. A ministry of reconciliation may begin around school issues but will undoubtedly broaden to include many aspects of the parent-youth relationship.

Simply by **showing an interest**, such as checking regularly about grades and inquiring about school issues, a minister can undergird the adolescent's school performance. Also, showing an interest demonstrates for the parents how to get more involved. Let the teens know that their work isn't being ignored.

Academic performance can often be improved by **having guided study halls or using tutors**. One church group provided tutors in an after-school program on a volunteer basis. Peer study groups provide perhaps the best program for tutoring and assisting. Frequently a Beta club or National Honor Society group will sponsor study groups. Of course, the academically struggling youngster must be motivated enough to want to learn and to trust a peer for help. Ministers can stimulate that motivation and provide space in the church for such programs.

Cheating and copying homework seems to be on the increase in some school systems. Not only does this rob students of learning opportunities, it sets a pattern and agenda that is detrimental to the work and school system. A clear system of reprimands and punishment may stop cheating at the time but cannot be expected to eliminate future cheating. Students will need positive reinforcement to back up and learn what was missed. They also need a positive approach to values education.

Assisting the parents and adolescents in **negotiating appropriate study place, time, and habits** is an important part of the ministry to the entire family. Since most ministers spend a good portion of their own time in study, perhaps they can share their personal style. It sometimes helps to talk about self-discipline and the capacity to do what one knows is best even when the playful child in all of us is tempted to goof off. Encourage the parents to provide an adequate place; offer space at the church.

General academic problems go hand in hand with low self-esteem. As a minister assists the adolescent in **finding a positive self-image**, academic crises will wane. Young people who feel accepted by God and blessed by the representatives of God have more energy, ambition, and joy to bring into the classroom. Self-formation is a continuous process and involves sustained attention from the minister.

Perhaps the best researched and most productive counseling approach to academic problems is **using behavior modification**. Set it up as a consistent, clear, personalized system of rewards and punishments. Dialogue with the adolescent, the school, and the parents for a broad base of support. Recall the four areas of response (from chapter 4): responses can (1) reward good behavior while ignoring bad behavior, (2) take away a privilege and motivate by grief, (3) initiate punishment and motivate by pain, or (4) lift a restriction and motivate by relief. Behavior modification systems will frequently need further adjustments after they are implemented. At first the monitoring may need to be daily and involve each teacher and the parents. As the system progresses, the adolescent needs to assume more responsibility for reporting on his or her own behavior. The ultimate goal is to internalize the control system so that the adolescent can face new challenges with only limited assistance.

While peer and school problems are a normal part of adolescent development, parents should not underreact. Often parents close their eyes to such issues until the problems become severe. A minister who notices a problem will do well to call it to the attention of the family and seek to deal with it before it becomes unmanageable. Spotting peer and school problems in the molehill phase of development frequently means that limited responses can bring lasting results. When academic problems go unattended during early adolescence, they are all but impossible to address effectively during high school. Likewise, unresolved early-adolescent peer maladjustments lay the foundations for crises of major proportion during middle and late adolescence. Even when the church can't directly assist, ministers can call attention to the problems and encourage families to seek counseling.

8

Depression and Suicide

Depression is such a normal part of the growing-up process that detecting severe depression in adolescents becomes difficult. Adolescents, like children and adults, are likely to become depressed at some point in their lives. Every time someone feels down isn't a crisis. However, when the depression becomes so heavy as to impair the ability to function, it has definitely reached the crisis stage. Someplace along the range between joy and depression a point is crossed and a crisis begins. And although depression is not the only factor in understanding the etiology of suicide in adolescents, it is perhaps the most common.

In the survey made for this book of the needs of young people for pastoral care, depression and suicide ranked among the very lowest of needs to be assessed, perhaps because they are not extensive problems. While 41 percent of ministers surveyed said depression was a high or urgent need only 33 percent felt that suicide was a high or urgent need Twenty percent said there was little or no need for pastora care to youth in the area of depression, and 40 percent said there was a low or nonexistent need for pastoral care to avoid teenage suicide. While it is estimated that around 400,000 adolescents attempt suicide annually in the United States, most youth ministers were hard pressed to name any youngsters they knew who had tried to kill themselves. Exact figures may be unobtainable because many attempts are not reported and others are listed as accidents. Ministers need to be more alert for potential crises in this area.

Figures do not begin to tell the painful story of depressed and suicidal adolescents. Not all depressions lead to suicide; not all suicides are prompted by depression. However, depression is undoubtedly the greatest single factor in pushing an adolescent toward self-destruction. We will discuss factors in adolescent depression and responses to depressed adolescents and then the dynamics of suicide. Pastoral care responses to those who are contemplating suicide conclude this chapter.

Adolescent Depression

Mild depression in adolescents is a common symptom and may be associated with a number of maladjustments and stress reactions. Knowing when depression is a normal part of an adolescent's adjustment to life and when it is severe and points to the need for crisis management is a crucial skill. Basically, when the depression has a negative effect on the adolescent's relationships and ability to function at home, school, work, or play, the depression deserves to be treated. Certainly, any time the depression is accompanied by suicidal gestures or ideation, the adolescent needs professional treatment. Depression may mask itself in several ways, and while no single behavioral change need be viewed with alarm, a cluster of symptoms usually indicates severe depression.

Depressed adolescents typically become inactive, drop out of peer relationships, spend large amounts of time alone, barricade themselves in their room, and escape into television (most likely something like MTV), music, or reading. Depressed adolescents show little initiative and project an "I don't care" attitude toward much of life. There is likely to be either a loss of appetite or a preoccupation with eating, especially bingeing on junk food. Likewise, either lack of sleep or too much sleep can denote a depression. Generally there is a lack of physical exercise and a decreased energy level, marked by frequent complaints of being tired. Depressed adolescents do not think clearly and are less perceptive of events in the world around them. They draw into themselves socially and cease to function productively at school or at work.

Adolescent depression comes from a wide range of possibilities. Certainly, heredity and personality type seem to play a large role in why some persons become more depressed than others. Internal factors such as physical illness and hormonal imbalances need to be checked out by a physician. Nevertheless, it seems that many causes of depression are external. Since early detection is important in treating adolescents with depression, the minister should follow up on all indications of problems. Consider causes of depression such as a sense of rejection, a major disappointment, or a recent loss. Any disappointment for a teenager, such as not getting a job or not making a team or not getting first chair in the band tryouts, can precipitate a depression or worsen an already existing depressive state.

Depression is a normal part of a grief reaction for adolescents, as it is for adults. When assessing a depressed youngster, ask about the death or loss of family members and close friends. Grief can also result from a recent move and the resulting uprooting from one's peer group. Another factor is the loss of a relationship from being excluded from a clique or being rejected from a valued peer group. Don't assume that the depressed adolescent became depressed *as* an adolescent. Check out childhood symptomatology to differentiate between normal adjustment-disorder depression and pathological depression.

Some forms of depression may be masked by various forms of delinquency and acting out.[1] When accompanied by feelings of powerlessness and hopelessness, depression leads to actions that may be self-destructive. Adolescents who are overwhelmed by a sense of failure may have eruptive episodes characterized by extreme impulsiveness. This type of deep depression is not as often related to a variety of stressors but is more the reflection of an affective disorder.

Pastoral Approaches with Depressed Teens

Sustaining, the process of walking alongside, is vital in responding to depression. The minister needs first of all to "be there" for the depressed young person. However, other elements of the pastoral perspective, discussed in chapter 2 come into consideration. For instance, there is a time for confronting the distortions that might lead one to be depressed. Likewise, there is a time for reconciling depressed persons with their community (peers and family). Since depression usually makes decision-making more difficult, the informing and guiding function can be expected to be a part of the process. This is particularly true toward the end of counseling. Of course, ultimately healing the depression is the long-range goal.

Some methods that have been helpful with depressed youngsters may not be in the standard repertoire of most youth ministers' methods of intervention. However, with careful supervision from trained pastoral supervisors and other professionals, one can begin to employ these techniques. Many pastors have had at least an introduction to pastoral care, and more than a few have had clinical training and will be ready to respond at a deeper level of counseling.

Build rapport. In working with depressed adolescents, extra attention needs to be given to the rather nonspecific characteristics of the relationship. Depressed adolescents can be even more difficult and resistant than those with behavior disorders. One needs to take time to build a durable counseling relationship. Warmth, empathy, and congruence are hallmarks of an effective counseling relationship with all persons but are particularly important in dealing with depressed teenagers.

Don't come on too strong. An aggressive, intense relationship may frighten a depressed adolescent and cause him or her to withdraw even more. Sensitive, supportive caring on a regular but brief basis is better for building the relationship.

Get them to do something. Activity is an important step in overcoming depression. While many persons will want to wait until they feel like participating in something and thus never get around to being involved, adolescents who can force themselves into action find that the depression lessons and new feelings evolve. Basically, they act their way into new feelings rather than feeling their way into acting differently.

Music helps. Music is the language in which many teens address their mood issues. Just as Saul was soothed by David's playing the lyre, many adolescents identify with and find release through music. While certain music addresses their depression, other music suggests new feelings. Body movements, exercise, and dancing can also facilitate mood shifts.

Try cognitive therapy. This has been found to be particularly successful with depressed persons and quite applicable to adolescents.[2] The basic tenet of cognitive therapy with depressed adolescents is simply to correct the false perceptions that can cause their depression. Adolescents are likely to have distorted interpretations of events in their environment. For example, a youngster might perceive another adolescent's behavior as rejection and then conclude, "If he [or she] doesn't like me, I'm not worth anything." Thinking "I'm not worth anything" leads to depression. The basic approach of cognitive therapy is to evaluate, through mutual logical reflection, both the data and the conclusions drawn from the data. The therapist assists the adolescent in questioning the data and in looking at alternative ways of interpreting the data. The counselor assists the depressed person in identifying errors in thinking. This is often enough to disprove depressive notions. For example, after evaluation, the youngster feeling depressed might conclude, "He [or she] was probably worried about something and didn't even see me. People still like me. I'm OK!"

Identify and externalize anger. Traditionally, this has worked well for depressed persons. Discussing the causes of the anger is also productive. Expressing the anger through actions such as pounding on a chair or stomping or expressive dancing to music has been less productive with adolescents than with adults, but assisting adolescents with dramatic expressions of their anger has been particularly helpful in depressive situations. This includes their writing out a small play or drama and then acting it out themselves with peers taking various roles. While extremely depressed adolescents may be reluctant to participate in these more active forms of expressing their frustrations, even those who watch seem to benefit.

Adolescent Suicide

As we turn our attention to adolescent suicide it is important to address a common myth. Ministers and youth workers have said to me, "I understand that teenagers who talk about suicide won't do it, and those who don't talk about it are the ones who try it." That dangerous falsehood may lead persons to be unresponsive to suicide talk and to overlook strong hints of suicidal ideation. Any time a teenager openly discusses or offers even veiled conversation about self-destruction, he or she needs to be treated with caution. It is better to err and take such a person too seriously (and be told that you have done so) than to pass lightly over a cry for help.

Most adolescents give clues; however, no two adolescent suicide cases are identical. Some factors in addition to depression that need to be considered in the assessment of a young person's potential for suicide include hopelessness, detachment, loneliness, grief, modeling, presuicidal behavior, and substance abuse. Each of these in and of themselves do not necessarily denote serious self-destructive thoughts, but when three or more are found together extreme caution needs to be exercised and suicide ideations need to be checked out by the minister or the counselor. If a person does not have professional training in dealing with suicidal teenagers, a referral for professional help should be offered immediately. However, one needs to be careful not to give the impression of abandoning the teen and bailing out. Reassure the youngster that your care will continue undiminished but that you are bringing in a professional counselor to assist the team. It is always prudent never to exceed one's limits and capabilities in counseling; this is even more imperative when dealing with suicidal tendencies in young people.

Hopelessness. Hopelessness seems to prevail in the lives of adolescents who finally despair to the point of contemplating suicide. Because adolescents live in the here and now, future hope is difficult for them even when they are not depressed. However, when depressed, feeling positive about the future seems almost absurd to many of them. Because of their perception that time is moving so slowly, long-range help seems of little value. In a similar fashion, because the depression tends to isolate them from peers, they feel hopeless about getting help from a friend. Generally, cognitive distortions about their environment feed this hopelessness. Many times they have given up on themselves and have a personal sense of hopelessness. In the first place they do not feel adequate to deal with the crisis, and in the second place they do not feel worthwhile or loved by other persons.

Detachment. Adolescents who have attempted suicide frequently report several weeks or even months of detached and withdrawn behavior. When asked "Who is your best friend?" they often cannot come up with anyone or they occasionally mention someone who lives many miles away and with whom they have not had recent contact. Although they live in the same house with siblings, parents, and other relatives, they describe their relationships with these persons as quite detached. Detachment at school can mean moving through an entire school day without speaking a full sentence to any other person, adolescent or adult. When talking with a detached adolescent, if other characteristics are present, suicide needs to be earnestly considered until ruled out as one of their alternatives.

Loneliness. Loneliness, while very similar to detachment, is more than a sense of lack of contact with persons. A lonely adolescent may have contact but perceives the contact to be meaningless. Lonely adolescents feel unloved by parents and peers. Loneliness is a perception of the lack of meaningful attachment to any significant other. One youngster may be very lonely in the midst of a crowd; another, who is living in solitude, may not be lonely because she or he has a preconceived sense of attachment to those who are not physically present.

Grief. Perhaps the most frequent precipitating event in adolescent suicide ideation and attempts is grief over a lost boyfriend or girlfriend. This is particularly true for middle adolescents whose identity formation has stagnated or delayed and who thus find their primary identity in belonging with the significant other. Adults frequently underestimate the pain and grief in the broken love relationships of adolescents. To the adolescent the rejection of losing a boyfriend or girlfriend is as painful as an adult experiencing a divorce. In despair and anger, shunned teenage lovers frequently turn to suicide. There has been some romanticizing of the relationship of lost love and suicide both in classical literature and in popular media portrayals of teenage life. Any time a breakup occurs in an adolescent dating relationship, caring adults need to be on the lookout for other symptoms and assist in processing the grief.

Modeling. There seems to·be a follow-the-leader effect when one adolescent in a community attempts suicide. Afterward, the others in the group are at greater risk. Suicide pacts are not uncommon. While studies are inconclusive, evidence suggests that adolescent suicides portrayed in the movies and television, particularly in urban settings, tend to precipitate attempts or at least push over the edge those adolescents who have already been contemplating suicide. When adolescents view suicide-related films, it is best that they have an opportunity to discuss their own thoughts and feelings with their parents or trained adult leaders. Adolescents, like adults, are more likely to attempt suicide if the pattern has been established in a previous generation by a relative who chose self-destruction as a way of escaping a problem.

Presuicidal Behavior. Adolescents who are seriously contemplating suicide will frequently begin to make ready for their departure. They give away prized possessions and present sentimental objects to friends, lovers, or even their parents. One young man decided to sell his most prized possession, a reconstructed automobile. Another left several trophies with a friend. Another returned pictures to an old girlfriend. Another kind of presuicidal behavior is saying good-bye; this may take the form of talking about going on a trip or discussing being gone. Tidying up can also be a clue. Sometimes adolescents will straighten up their room, clean their clothes, and put things in place with unusual attention to detail.

Like adults, some presuicidal adolescents are less depressed. This new cheerfulness may lull others into a false security. It seems as if a brief interlude of happiness comes from having finally made the decision.

Obviously, suicide statements and suicide notes are serious presuicidal behavior. Not all adolescents leave a note or even take time to say good-bye; however, many do leave a note in which frequently they ask forgiveness and express their love to certain persons. Many notes are similar in nature. A suicide note left by one young man was taken by a group of peers in another state to be the note of their friend. The note read:

> *Dear Steve, I'm sorry for what I have done but Robert and Mom made me think. Will your mom still have wanted us to be friends? I don't know. Tell Missy I love her and I hope she can still pass Science. Make sure you never be as dumb as I have been. Make friends and don't let them play that tape before my funeral. Friends, Jay.*[3]

This young man wrote at least five notes to other persons, as well as a recorded tape message. His note to his mother is particularly characteristic.

> *I'm sorry for what I've put you through. I am empty. I just can't face my friends. I want the entire ninth grade invited to my funeral and at the funeral, and not before, play this tape. Please don't play it before if you love me. Also have Tommy fly down if at all possible. Love you. I'm scared. Jay.*[4]

Suicide notes can express love, anger, grief, or shame. Whatever feelings seem to be pent up and inexpressible in life are expressed by the act of death·

Substance Abuse. A dramatic increase in drug and alcohol consumption is a factor in nonfatal suicidal attempts more than in either suicide completions or natural deaths.[5] Therefore, new involvement in drugs and alcohol as well as other significant changes in personality may be "acting out" behaviors that are signs of suicidal thoughts. They are disguised cries for help. Since many completed suicide attempts begin as cries for help, they must be taken seriously. One can never conclude that someone is only halfheartedly attempting suicide and is therefore at less risk.

Pastoral Care and Counseling with Teenage Suicide Crises

The interventions and responses that follow focus on the minister's role and are not intended as a comprehensive discussion for a suicide intervention team.

Caring, getting involved, and forming a primary bond are the most significant ways to help adolescents choose against suicide as an option. However, in befriending suicidal teenagers there are many potential barriers. We must do more than speak of our friendship. We must also **listen to them** in a way that signals our deep care and respect for them as persons. We need to be cautious not to minimize their concerns. Adolescents may first discuss minor issues to test the level of care before revealing serious problems. Communicate to them the depth of your caring.

While taking them seriously, caring, and listening to them are the beginning stages, these responses by no means resolve the suicidal crisis. **Help adolescents ground themselves in reality.** Your attention may give them hope in the short range, but in the long range they need to identify their problems, express the repressed negative emotions around those problems, evaluate the reality of their interpretations and conclusions, and select an appropriate alternative for resolving the problems. Frequently in their darkest moments, adolescents doubt that we care for them; they also distort the intensity of their problems. One very depressed fifteen-year-old girl overheard her parents discussing a financial matter and, without further checking, came to the distorted conclusion that money matters were much more serious than they actually were. Such distortions are not an uncommon basis for actually attempting suicide.

After adolescents have checked out the reality of their interpretations and their understanding of the crisis from those involved, they can express their feelings about the real situation. While they may want to ventilate feelings about their distorted conclusions, only correcting their perceptions, and not mere ventilation, will ultimately relieve these feelings.

After a suicide attempt, the ministry of reconciliation can help reunite a youth with both the peer group and the family. The suicidal adolescent may have multiple broken relationships that need mending. A long-range goal of pastoral counseling is to **facilitate the building of community** and koinonia with the fellowship of the entire church.

Suicide is an individual phenomenon and involves the need to "send a message" to significant others. As an expression of anger it attempts to get even with or hurt someone. Usually this person is a family member or close friend; however, this anger is more likely a symptom not to be viewed in isolation.[6] A professional who is assisting an adolescent with suicidal ideations should **include all family members** who are living in the household who will come for counseling. Even when the parents are no longer living together, they both need to be included. It is not uncommon to find that the adolescent's behavior is actually being subtly encouraged by someone in the family system. Some call this "psychic homicide"[7]; the family not only expects the suicide but begins to participate in helping make it possible by leaving the means of suicide available. The susceptible adolescent seems to feel that death will serve a sacrificial purpose and actually save the family.

When seeing the entire family, decisions about hospitalizing the suicidal adolescent must be made. Most state laws require that someone who attempts suicide must be hospitalized. Adolescents whose attempts are private and perhaps in secluded areas are more serious about dying than those whose attempts are made around the family or peers, where they are likely to be found in time. However, neither case should be taken lightly. Engaging the family system helps in discovering the relationships between the adolescent and each family member as well as in assessing the family as a system. Of particular significance are the communication patterns, the methods of resolving conflict, the level of stress on the family, the capacity of the family to give and receive forgiveness, affirmation, and blessings, and the family's expectations and rules. A family history obviously is needed. The teenager's suicide attempt may be an extreme reaction to dysfunction in the family system. In fact, one study found that after the suicide of a family member, several families reported "that post-suicidal family relationships may actually have been strengthened."[8] This is not to say that these families welcomed the suicide. Suicidal death compounds and confuses the family's grief reaction considerably.[9] It is paramount to examine all family dynamics when counseling an adolescent with suicide ideations.

Depressed and suicidal adolescents' resolve to live is strengthened if you **give them an opportunity to tell their life story**. Getting them in touch with their history and letting them verbalize their own significant events seems to overpower some of the feelings of detachment and loneliness. Acceptance or rejection from grandparents seems to be of considerable importance to a number of depressed teenagers. Letting them discuss conflicts with their parents and their relationship to parents and stepparents is vital. As they share their history, it is helpful to assist them in interpreting the dynamics of their life through the gospel story. For example, the loneliness of Jesus in the Garden of Gethsemane might be related to their description of their own sense of isolation and loneliness.

For adolescents who see suicide as an escape from an intolerable situation, **seek alternative ways to resolve the pain**. Adolescents have difficulty seeing alternatives for their crisis and need the assistance of ministers and counselors to generate sensible choices. Guiding them during the time of selecting one or more alternatives means supporting their right to make decisions. They also need sustaining encouragement in actually attempting to implement a desirable alternative. A white adolescent youth who had attempted suicide remained distant from the hospital staff and myself for some time. When he gained enough trust to tell his story, it seemed he had opted for suicide as a way of relieving his family of the shame of having him and of his guilt. No one particular event caused the guilt; rather, he felt a general sense of guilt about himself. The major turning point in his journey was realizing that there were alternatives for dealing with his guilt and pain. He could feel as good or better than he fantasized he would feel in suicide. Helping adolescents know that suicide is not a glamorous, painless, easy solution can assist them in deciding for life's alternatives. Dealing directly with shame, guilt, and the disappointment of broken relationships is not hopeless from a theological perspective.

As the adolescent's depression, detachment, loneliness, and guilt improve, she or he is briefly at greatest risk for an actual suicide attempt. Be especially careful to **take precautions to protect adolescents from themselves** at this time. They may need to be hospitalized on a unit where suicide precautions can be ensured. Do not leave them alone and unsupervised for long periods of time. Protective precautions not only prevent an accidental or impulsive suicide but show adolescents the deep sense of esteem and care in which they are held.

A significant factor in long-range health can be to **bring closure on the suicide ideation**. There comes a time when the teenager has moved beyond thoughts of suicide, but the family and peers may continue to see a "suicide risk." Give a sense of acceptance, a willingness not only to forgive and forget but to move on with life in a graceful manner. One teen mused a year later, "I can't believe I did a thing like that [attempted suicide]. I wish people would stop talking about it."

Assisting depressed and suicidal adolescents to move on with life is basically an invitation to a lifelong spiritual journey. While it is possible that a large percentage of the population has thought of suicide at one point or another in their adolescence, certainly not all have attempted or taken that contemplation seriously. All do need to be accepted into the community of faith and nurtured along the spiritual journey. They need to live life with the affirmation that they are persons of worth, with the hope that by the help of God they can not only transform their environment but reshape the future. They are called to live, to love, and to relate to self, life, and God in a manner described in John's Gospel as "abundant living."

9

Substance Abuse

"It's not that which goes into the mouth but that which comes out of the mouth that defiles a person," one youth snapped. He went on to proclaim that it was no worse for him to smoke pot than it was for his father to have a martini every evening after work. Adolescents regularly point to the biblical teaching of moderation on the use of alcohol and the practice of Jesus to use wine as they attempt to build a case for their own abuse. Seldom, however, do they quote from Ephesians 5:18, "Do not get drunk with wine," or from Leviticus 11:34 or John 2:10 or Luke 21:34 or Romans 13:13 or any of the passages that speak of avoiding the abuse of substances. This chapter outlines some of the causes of substance abuse in adolescents including not just misuse of alcohol and drugs but also the misuse of food. Pastoral approaches to the abuse of alcohol and drugs are similar to ways of dealing with food abusers. Those who overeat and those who refuse to eat, like those who turn to alcohol and drugs, are attempting to cope with a variety of hurtful, shameful, painful emotions in the absence of a support system.

Alcohol and Other Drugs

While evidence pointed to a slight decline in 1987 in overall drug use among adolescents and young adults as well as in the use of cocaine, the United States still had the highest rate of illicit drug use of any country in the industrialized world.[1] According to one survey, over 50 percent of high school seniors had tried marijuana, and one in three had experimented with various illegal drugs. However, 87 percent of all high school seniors disapproved of experimentation with cocaine (a 7 percent decrease from 1986), and only 3 percent approved of regular cocaine use. By the time children reach thirteen, around 30 percent of boys and 23 percent of girls consume alcohol. Catholics, whites, northeasterners, and males are more likely to drink, and by age eighteen, 92 percent of boys and 73 percent of teenage girls are drinkers.[2]

Church leaders report major concern with a need for pastoral care to adolescents with alcohol and drug problems. Fifty-five percent of those responding to the survey made for this book felt a high or an urgent need for pastoral care to such young people. It was the most urgent problem, according to the survey, with 18 percent having said the need was urgent. Nevertheless, only 3 percent of those responding reported that their church does an excellent job in ministering to adolescents with alcohol and drug problems, while 28 percent reported that their church's ministry to adolescents with alcohol and drug problems was poor or nonexistent. Abuse is widespread, the need for ministry is high, and the responses of most churches are less than adequate. Understanding the reasons behind alcohol and drug abuse and having a basic knowledge of the effects of alcohol and drugs are the first steps in developing a ministry program.

Why Do Adolescents Take Drugs?

Adolescents with various levels of use and abuse described a multitude of motivations. Many adolescents cannot explain why they first used drugs, including alcohol, because of their lack of self-awareness and their lack of the dynamics affecting their lives. The comment "I just tried some one day, and I guess I liked it and then tried it some more" is typical of many early and middle adolescents who later get hooked on substance abuse. Alcohol and drugs become an alternative to boredom.

Excitement. Seeking excitement is the first motive that leads to substance abuse. Recreational users will frequently abuse at a party, and soon getting high becomes a regular first step to having fun. Every recipe for a good time begins with a bottle of booze or a joint or some pills. Richard Parsons, professor of pastoral counseling at Neumann College, attributes parent modeling as a major influence on adolescents who drink for entertainment and excitement.[3]

Escape. In addition to those seeking a good time, other adolescents turn to substance abuse as an escape from pain. In essence they are self-medicating. They want to escape depression or anxiety or timidity or anger or whatever unpleasant feeling dominates their lives. "I'm not good at talking to girls until I've had a couple of drinks," one young man confessed. "Smoking a few joints doesn't hurt anyone, and it helps me forget the arguing and fighting at home," said a distraught teenage girl. Adolescents escaping from the painful realities of their troubled world need crisis intervention and support even more than those who turn to drugs and alcohol for excitement. Those who escape are more likely to become addicts. In a double-barreled way, they are creating new problems through the substance abuse, while at the same time refusing to face current problems.

Experimentation. A third reason for turning to substance abuse is simply experimentation. Frequently, peer pressure will cause those who want to be included in a group or are lonely or are seeking acceptance to respond positively to the taunt, "Oh, come on and try some. It will be fun. Nobody will be hurt." Middle adolescents, especially in their stage of experimentation, are vulnerable to turning to drugs "just for the experience." Parents need to be careful not to panic and think their kid has a major drug or alcohol problem just because he or she has experimented once or twice. Obviously, one would wish that such experimentation were not a part of the adolescent experience, but experimentation is not addiction and is not on a level with regular use. Adolescents who experiment only occasionally can readily be turned from drugs with a positive peer group and supportive information about the dangers of drug use.

Inherited Disease. Personality difficulties, characterological disorders, and inherited addictive predispositions are a fourth factor in substance abuse. While conclusions are mixed on addiction as an inherited disease, it is known that infants whose mothers are addicts can be born addicted. As Derek Miller defines addiction—chronic intoxication produced by the repeated consumption of a drug—many adolescents become addicted after their parents have already done so.[4]

"Some scientists say that the search for a physiological basis for alcoholism is far enough along now that it will be found," says Enoch Jordis, director of the National Institute of Alcohol

Abuse and Alcoholism.[5] By studying adopted children whose biological parents were alcoholics, it has been learned that "the offspring of alcoholics are significantly more likely than other people to become alcoholics themselves regardless of whether their adoptive parents abuse alcohol."[6] She goes on to say that genetics is not the only question since over a third of all alcoholics have no family history of the disorder, and only from 30 to 40 percent of the sons of alcoholics have ever become alcoholics themselves. However, there are still many questions about this inherited addiction theory. While the medical debate rages on, the need remains urgent.

Anger. Angry rebellion is a fifth reason adolescents turn to drugs and substance abuse. They will often get drunk or get high as a way of getting even with their parents, a boyfriend, or a girlfriend. It is a way of escaping. When they do not know how to identify and confront their angry, hurt, disappointed feelings and are unable to think through the events in a productive manner, they will often turn to alcohol.

There are identifiable patterns of increased use with age. Adolescents might begin with occasional experimentation; however, the substances hold a seductive promise of effortless relief and pleasure without the struggle of active mastery or attempted coping.[7] As magical solutions continue to elude the adolescent, use of alcohol and other drugs becomes more recurrent until a chronic need for the drug-induced condition becomes traumatic. This progressive pattern of the use of alcohol and drugs is not determinism. It does not mean that once an adolescent experiments, he or she is doomed to addiction.

A New York State Department of Mental Hygiene study on adolescent illicit drug use concluded:

> Two additional factors that surface almost as strong for the use of other illicit drugs besides marijuana was the adolescent's closeness to parents and personality characteristics such as depression and poor school performance. In the probability of using illicit drugs other than marijuana, the lack of closeness to parents was almost as important as the fact that one's friends were using drugs.[8]

It appears that sex differences in junior and senior high students are not the major factors in patterns of alcohol and drug abuse. Girls are nearly as likely as boys to abuse both alcohol and drugs.[9]

Marijuana use seems to be on the decline in the United States according to the November 1987 *Harvard Medical School Mental Health Letter.* In a 1978 survey, 37 percent of high school seniors said they had smoked marijuana within the last seven days and 11 percent reported daily use. By 1986, the number who had smoked marijuana in the last thirty days had decreased to 23 percent, and the proportion of daily users had dropped to only 4 percent. While, in 1969, 20 percent of high school seniors had used marijuana and, by 1979, 60 percent reported that they had, by 1985 the figure was only 54 percent. In 1985, 85 percent of high school seniors disapproved of marijuana and 70 percent said its use was risky, while in 1978, only 35 percent said its use was risky. (See Figure 8.)

Whatever the cause, adolescents can be addicted to alcohol and drugs. After becoming addicted, they are in need of serious crisis intervention. Education, counseling, and support alone are not enough. Medical attention, usually as an inpatient, is most often also needed. Family counseling and a total systems approach based upon behavior modification principles is most effective in assisting the adolescent addict.

Figure 8. High school students and marijuana use.

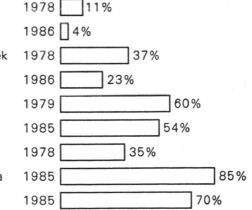

Daily use of marijuana	1978	11%
	1986	4%
Smoked marijuana within week	1978	37%
	1986	23%
Have tried smoking marijuana	1979	60%
	1985	54%
Use of marijuana is risky	1978	35%
Disapprove of using marijuana	1985	85%
Use of marijuana is risky	1985	70%

The Church's Ministry with Adolescents Who Use Drugs

Preventive programs based on accurate information about alcohol, marijuana, and other illicit drugs and their effect on the human body and mind appear to be the best approach to adolescents. But although preventive programs serve as the best deterrent to involvement, a sufficient number of adolescents are in need of pastoral care and crisis intervention.

Preventive Measures

Because adolescents respond positively to peer counseling and group contexts, ministers should support the formation of Alateen groups alongside the Alcoholics Anonymous groups in the community. Ministers should support organizations like Students Against Drunk Drivers. And ministers should work with communities and schools in developing broad-based chemical-dependency education programs.

Some church groups have assisted parents and children in forming covenants and pledges that there will be no drinking and driving. If adolescents are drinking, they can call their parents to come and pick them up without a hassle. Other groups have found that parents whose adolescents wished to experiment with alcohol have been successful in educating their children about the use of alcohol and permitting them to experiment by tasting one drink in the presence of the parents. This gives the adolescent an out when encouraged to experiment by peers. They can say, "I tried it and I don't like it." Many parents still adhere to teaching total abstinence.

Since distance from one's parents is a causative factor, especially in illicit drug involvement, churches can assist in a preventive fashion by offering education programs that strengthen the overall family life within their congregations. Family life education programs that focus the need for quality family time together go a long way in creating an environment where alcohol and drug use is less likely to erupt.

Pastoral Care

Pastoral care issues are important in ministering to adolescent substance abusers, since depression, anxiety, and the inability to express anger frequently contribute to adolescent drug abuse. A minister who deals with those issues from a theological perspective can be of great assistance to the adolescent. Focusing on the adolescent's self-identity from a positive point of view will encourage the adolescent to find the strength to acknowledge the problem of substance abuse and seek further help.

Sustaining and guiding are significant factors in pastoral care of adolescent drug users. Sustaining the adolescent in the ongoing struggle may even mean being on call in an Alcoholics Anonymous contract fashion if the adolescent is tempted to return to the abuse. Contracts sustain the adolescent who is turning from regular use. Reconciliation is also an important factor of pastoral care with adolescent abusers. Reconciliation in the family system is usually needed. Frequently, the adolescent's relationships with church groups or other friends will be broken, and the minister can serve to facilitate reconciliation in both groups. Reconciliation with peers may mean that the minister serves as a bridge to introduce the former substance abuser into a new peer group and then assists in finding a new role and a new place in the Christian community. Adolescents who are regular abusers will frequently have limited social skills. Involving them in social skills groups and teaching them appropriate behavior can be an important part in reintegrating them in the peer group.

Family Issues

Several counseling issues surface with the adolescent who is a frequent user, abuser, or addict. First, the family must be assessed. If the parents are also substance abusers, a family systems intervention model is recommended. Treatment for all members of the family in the various programs of Alcoholics Anonymous should be used in conjunction with individual and family counseling. Perhaps one or more members of the system will need long-term institutionalization in a substance abuse rehabilitation center. However, such resident programs seem to be more effective with adults than adolescents. One study failed to find statistically significant differences in the outcome of outpatient treatment of delinquent drug abusers as over against inpatient treatment.[10]

Family structural issues must still be addressed by the counselor when the adolescent abuses drugs but the parents do not. When parents are nonabusers, family dynamics can be more powerful in assisting the adolescent through the process of becoming a nonabuser also. Structural issues that need to be dealt with are the family's ability to set and maintain appropriate limits and the family's commitment to spend regular quality time with the adolescent. Furthermore, the family needs to communicate to the adolescent that they are forming a covenant relationship. This is a particularly difficult issue because the adolescent is in the midst of a struggle for independence. Care and bondedness should not be confused with creating dependence. In the context of respect for the adolescent's personhood, such bondedness need not denote control.

Cognitive Issues

In addition to family issues, cognitive issues surface in counseling with adolescent drug and alcohol abusers. Frequently, adolescents will harbor a multitude of cognitive distortions about adolescents and about alcohol and drugs and their abuse. Such distortions might be in the area of **selective abstraction**, where they would say, "The only way I can have fun at a party is to get high." Another cognitive distortion, **overgeneralization**, might find its way in statements like "I stopped drinking for two days, so I know I can quit any time I want to" or "Nobody liked me and I never had any fun before I started using, and if I quit my friends will drop me." A third cognitive distortion, **magnification**, can be seen in relationship to substance abuse when the adolescent says something like "I do my most creative work with a little bit of help from the bottle" or "If I quit, it's going to push me over the limit, and I'll never be able to face the problems in my family."

All-or-nothing reasoning, another cognitive distortion, is frequent among adolescent abusers. They will say something like "I can't keep it all together unless I have a few drinks, and if I can't have a few drinks, I won't be able to do anything. I won't even graduate from school." Of course, adolescents personalize the drinking issue when they say, "I'll lose all my friends if I'm not drinking. Everybody's doing it, and they'll reject me if I don't go along." A final cognitive error, **superstitious thinking**, shows the almost magical distortion of some adolescents. "If I take a little bit of this stuff, I have powers beyond anything I can have without it. Just a few drags from the weed and I'm a social butterfly," they might say.

In counseling adolescents, one must be alert for cognitive distortions and confront youngsters with the need to examine the reality involved in their actual substance abuse. When they can see their mistakes in observation and information processing, they can then be led to discover for themselves ways of relating and functioning that do not involve substance abuse.

As Alcoholics Anonymous has successfully pointed out, admitting one is powerless and needs help from a Higher Power is an important step in recovery. The pastoral counselor is in a unique place to introduce the adolescent to the Higher Power. While a manipulative approach would do more damage than good, assisting the adolescent in beginning a sincere faith pilgrimage is a crucial step in long-term recovery from substance abuse. Furthermore, the pastoral counselor can assist the adolescent to deal with the guilt and grief issues that frequently accompany a pattern of abuse. Through honest forgiveness and seeking to clean up relationships and become reconciled with peers and family, the adolescent can find new meaning in life.

Behavior Modification

Behavior modification with adolescents who are substance abusers has been particularly successful when the rewards and tokens are uniquely tied to the adolescent's own values and aspirations. Motivation for treatment is an issue in all emotional problems of adolescents. However, in working with drugs and alcohol, the adolescent's motivation is a key factor before any behavior modification program can be implemented.[11] Furthermore, having the complete support of everyone in the adolescent's environment is necessary for a behavior modification program to work. For that reason, inpatient programs are usually most effective. However, when the schools, parents, church, and friends of an adolescent will al support that adolescent in behavior modification, an outpatient program can be successful. The actual rewards set up for abstinence and for attaining long-range and short-range behavior goals are not as important as the praise, affirmation, and relationships of peers and significant adults. Many times adolescents have been using the substance itself as a reward When drugs are replaced by more meaningful, less destructive rewards, adolescent behavior will improve.

For occasional abusers, meaningful family experiences and quality time with the same-sex parent frequently serve as the best reinforcement for not using drugs and alcohol. The pastoral counselor's role in such behavior modification is to form a contract that includes (1) confrontation of the dysfunctional behavior, (2) clear understanding of the desirable goals, and (3) tokens that support movement toward health. Being available at all times is important for all counseling with adolescents under stress; however, it is crucial for abusers (as it is for those at risk for suicide).

Theological Issues

A central theological issue for counseling with adolescent abusers is that of **personhood**. When personhood can be rooted in a firm understanding of the importance of all humanity, as seen in the creation and incarnation, an adolescent finds a new sense of positive self-worth—a natural high. Assisting adolescents in finding a personhood based in Christian theology undergirds them to avoid the crises of substance abuse.

A further theological issue, **calling**, or purpose in life, assists adolescents in dealing with abuse issues. As the pastoral counselor seeks to uncover the purpose served by the drinking—for example, control of anxiety, overcoming shyness, experimentation—alternatives are explored. The minister seeks to guide adolescents toward God's deeper purpose in life, to deal with those issues. Wayne Oates provides an excellent discussion of how identity and purpose can be grounded in the Christian faith in his classic volume *Christ and Selfhood.*

When the adolescent has used substance for relief of intrapsychic pain, an introduction to the spiritual journey provides a more productive alternative. While systematic desensitization and relaxation techniques are not necessarily related to prayer and meditation, they can be. When used in conjunction with Christian prayer and meditation, they have been powerful therapeutic tools in assisting adolescents to feel at peace with themselves and God. Some have reported that their meditative experiences in prayer exceed those which previously resulted from use of drugs.

Food Abuse

As with other forms of substance abuse, the factors involved in abuse of food are complex. Anxiety, experimentation, modeling of peers and parents, power control issues, and lack of self-esteem have all been linked with both anorexia and obesity. The Bible regularly includes gluttony in its list of abuses, although refusing to eat can be taken as religious commitment; fasting is an expression of discipline, and prayer is one of the spiritual gifts. However, gluttony and fasting are both neglected in most Protestant theology.

One of the slanderous statements made about Jesus by those seeking to discredit him was that he came eating and drinking: "Behold, a glutton and a drunkard" (Matt. 11:19). Abuses of food and alcohol have long been seen as problems.

Not all preoccupation with dieting and not all obesity are signs of emotional disorders; obviously, a variety of genetic and biological factors must be taken into consideration. Nevertheless, among adolescents, particularly adolescent girls, a number of eating disorders deserve attention.

The decade of the eighties has seen an explosion of research into eating disorders. Anorexia nervosa, not eating to the point that it impairs one's health, and bulimia, binge eating and then self-induced vomiting that jeopardizes health, receive most of the attention. While there are still many questions to be researched, it seems that persons with eating disorders frequently experience a serious deficit in their ability to recognize and express a variety of feelings. This is most pronounced in bulimic patients.[12]

Pastoral Care and Counseling Responses

As pastoral counselors attempt to aid patients with eating disorders in sharing a variety of feelings, they not only assist in identifying feelings but also in directing them toward appropriate targets. Teens need help in engaging the range of intensity of these feelings. Assisting adolescents in accepting their feelings will increase their self-esteem as well as facilitate their integration into peer group and family structures. Furthermore, the pastoral counselor can model affective communication by the way he or she shares and identifies feelings in the counseling session.

Cognitive distortions and misinterpretations of body image seem to be a consistent factor for food abusers. This is particularly true for anorexic patients. Thomas C. Todd, director of the Marriage and Family Therapy and Training Program in Bristol, Connecticut, has pointed to research indicating that combining cognitive therapy and family therapy has been particularly helpful with anorexic patients. Characteristic distortions are seen in statements like, "The only way I can be in control is through eating" (selective abstraction) or "I used to be of normal weight, and I wasn't happy, so I know gaining weight isn't going to make me feel better" (overgeneralization) or "Gaining five pounds would push me over the limit" (magnification).[13] As the pastoral counselor attempts to combine family and cognitive therapy, he or she needs to be particularly mindful of distortions that are reinforced by the family, by family myths, or by family rules. Direct confrontation is frequently resisted by further "not eating" behavior. Therefore, assisting the adolescent to uncover cognitive distortions through examining the evidence seems to work more productively.

The concept of self seems to be a central issue for those who abuse food. The self is viewed as an object of disdain, and self-esteem suffers significantly. Pastoral counseling with food abusers, as with other substance abusers, can focus on self-esteem issues and one's relationship with God and the people of God. Because self-esteem issues are so important, some researchers indicate that females should counsel female substance abusers for the benefit of the modeling on the part of the counselor.[14]

Separation and autonomy issues also surface in adolescents with eating disorders. Some obese persons seem to fear attachments with members of the opposite sex and use obesity as a symbolic layer of insulation to create distance between themselves and others. Anorexics who are preoccupied with their thinness seem to be attempting to thwart the developmental maturity process in order to remain a child and not have to leave their parents. This desire to retreat from maturity may also be a desire to avoid emergent sexuality that might be seen as a threat to relationships to parents.[15] When separation and autonomy are central issues, the development of a greater degree of self-identity and differentiation from the family through family therapy methods and the addressing of the anxiety through theological and pastoral approaches seem to work quite well. Seeking independence is encouraged. In a context of trust and faith in the sustaining power of God, relationship with families and peers can be less fearful and even a source of joy.

Because of the control and power issues in eating disorders, behavioral methods seem to have inconsistent results. This is especially true when the behavioral treatment has been mechanistically misapplied. There may be short-term results but long-term change does not happen, because of the presence of underlying issues.[16]

From a pastoral counseling point of view, encouraging food abusers to have a positive respect for their body as a creation and gift from God goes hand in hand with a positive formation of the sense of self. From a Christian perspective one is acceptable in any body, regardless of color or size. This assertion can be used to confront adolescent preoccupations with an idealized image and a fear of not having an acceptable body.

Referring teens for medical help is an important ministry. Sometimes the family fails to see the seriousness of the issue. Not everyone who is thin or everyone who is outside some "ideal" weight is in need of counseling. One rule of thumb for identifying anorexic girls is to figure twenty pounds for each foot of height and five pounds for each inch above five feet. For example, a five-foot five-inch female of average build could weigh 125—one hundred pounds for the five feet and another twenty-five pounds for the five inches. Anorexia would be considered an issue if her body weight were to drop in a quick period of time below 90 percent of that weight—to 112 pounds or less. For example, one youngster lost 13 percent of her body weight in three weeks after breaking up with her boyfriend, a typical attachment anxiety issue. For someone hospitalized for anorexia, the 90-percent point is a likely goal for discharge. If an anorexic girl drops to 80 percent of her body weight (to 100 pounds for our 125-pound example), severe physical complications can set in; there can be a stopping of the growth hormones, and the menstrual cycle may stop. More than 15 percent *above* normal body weight can also create health problems by putting additional strain on the heart and circulatory system. In general, healthy relationships with family and peers and significant others make maintaining a healthy body less stressful

10

The Churches Respond

The Christian church stands in a unique position in Western culture to respond to the needs of adolescents in crisis. Their questions about the meaning of life, their confusion around moral issues, and their searching for personal groundedness offer faith groups an unparalleled opportunity. While limitations exist, the church cannot neglect her responsibility to teens. Many ministers who responded to the questionnaire mentioned in the introduction detailed not only their regular ministry with youth but also special pastoral care and counseling programs. Pastoral counselors, chaplains, pastors, and youth ministers shared some basic insights on caring for teenagers in crisis that will be summarized here.

One veteran youth minister now in training as a professional pastoral counselor shared an insightful thought.

> The contemporary needs of youth are not met through quick-fix solutions and campfire-brand spirituality. Youth need adults who genuinely care but also have skills in listening, communicating, and *modeling* the age-old story of God's love in Jesus Christ. Youth need strong bridges of relationship built to weather the storms of time in order to help them live securely and to believe authentically in the concepts of faith, hope, love, and grace. We cannot out-entertain the world of Bruce Springsteen, Michael Jackson, and Madonna, but with skill born of training and grace conceived in Christ we can care for youth in crisis.

Why should ministers get involved with adolescents in crisis in the first place? "Aren't there enough medical and psychiatric treatment programs to care for them?" one parent asked.

Admittedly, there are barriers to the church's involvement in caring for our young people in crisis, and some people may argue that the church should not get involved. However, in the long run the reasons for getting involved outweigh the limitations.

Barriers to Overcome

There are numerous reasons given by other professionals and excuses given by ministers for not getting involved in the care of adolescents in crisis. Beyond the typical brush-off are some substantial limitations of clergy in the church. Some ministers will say "I just don't relate well to teenagers" or "The adults are the backbone of this church" or "I haven't time to concentrate on adolescents" or, simply, "Not many young people come to our church." More serious questions are raised around other issues.

Lack of Training. The training required for responding to the needs of adolescents in crisis may exceed the training provided the average minister. Unless a minister has had opportunity for specialized supervision in counseling and crisis ministry, he or she may soon find that the crisis is overwhelming. While no one can be informed in all of the areas that confront adolescents in crisis, ministers can become knowledgeable about basic issues such as adolescent identity formation, sexual crisis, and adolescent faith questions. Furthermore, even ministers who lack specific training in depth counseling are likely to have some training in how to make a referral and in paving the way for someone to seek professional help.

Lack of Time. The demands on ministers' time are already heavy, and responding to teenagers in crisis can consume large additional blocks of time and energy. "Crisis ministry will take away from the other needs of my congregation," complained one minister. This is true. A minister is a busy professional, but so are many others. Usually, time considerations are a matter of a lack of priorities. If ministers cannot themselves deal with young people, they need to seek additional staff or train lay volunteers who have the time and desire to minister with adolescents in crisis. Churches who do not find time for teenagers will not have the continued presence of young people in their church. Even though larger churches have special youth ministers, it is not enough to turn over all of the crisis needs of adolescents to that person. In order to remain sensitive to the needs of youth, the pastor must stay involved at some level. Usually this means, at a minimum, hospital visitation, some limited family counseling, and being present at major youth functions like retreats. "Let the minister of youth or the minister of activities do that" is an inadequate response.

Lack of Trust. "Ministers are not always trusted by teenagers, for a variety of reasons," proclaimed a high school counselor. Typically some teens are in a process of revolting against external authority. This includes not only parents, teachers, and "the cops" but also institutions like the church. More than a few are rebelling against God. As one respondent from Hawaii confessed, "It's a real problem in getting youth to see my church as a viable resource." Admittedly, the polarization of American culture into the secular and the sacred does create a barrier for reaching out to distrustful adolescents. Nevertheless, during a time of crisis, adolescents are more willing to accept a caring response from any source. One cannot assume that all of those outside the church are rebelling against the church. We need to overcome stereotypic projections on their part. Ministers who care during the time of crisis will be seen as a valued resource.

Ministers are not always trusted by mental health and legal professionals. Because a few ministers have abused privileges in visitation or created further apprehension by a lack of integrity or training, some professionals are reluctant to welcome ministers onto the helping team. However, if one takes the time to get to know resistant professionals and relate to them from a clearly theological position, respect and rapport among professionals can be earned. Achieved relationships are more durable in a time of crisis than expecting power to be ascribed simply because of one's role

Lack of Money. "Small churches have limited means and cannot afford the resources to specialize in ministry to youth in crisis," complained an exacerbated pastor. Even though the number of adolescents may be small, their needs are just as important as those of adults. And although small churches often have limited resources, the resources of the wider community are available if someone will take the time to get involved and build an adequate referral system. In reality, many small churches provide growth opportunities for the involvement of young members, who play the piano, serve as ushers, or teach a children's study. Limited resources can become an opportunity for some youngsters to "find themselves by losing themselves" in service. Large churches have less need for young people to be involved in leadership positions, but some do involve teens in mission work to the community.

Lack of Continuity. A final barrier to a minister's involvement with adolescents in crisis is the transitory nature of many ministers' lives. In some denominations, ministers who work with teenagers and others average less than two years with a given congregation. Moving so often disrupts the relationships needed in times of crisis. Ministers who are serious about the needs of adolescents should work through appointment systems so that they stay at least four or five years with a given congregation. Ten to twenty years is ideal. It takes perhaps two years to build enough rapport in a youth group for the teens to begin to open up and share their deepest concerns. Building trust is not a short-term process. Ministers who "stay in the trenches" can minister much more effectively in crisis.

Young people expect a lot of their minister. Many of us may be tempted to respond like "the preacher" in the comic strip "Kudzu." A youngster suggests that being a preacher must be really hard, recites a long list of expectations, and concludes with people watching, waiting for one false move, one sign of human frailty they can jump on. "I don't know how you handle it!" The minister's reply? "I stay home a lot."[1]

Avoiding demands is unacceptable. One minister cautioned, "Remember, they are watching you." Modeling is an important part of building a relationship with adolescents in crisis. If they do not respect and trust an adult, little can be accomplished.

Reasons for Pastoral Care with Youth

For a variety of reasons, ministers should respond to the needs of adolescents in crisis. While they are certainly one part of a caring team and must be careful to develop professional interdependence with other professionals in the community, they are greatly remiss if they neglect their role in the process.

Clergypersons are in an unparalleled professional position by having a relationship with all members of the family. Because of the minister's **access across generation lines**, she or he is more likely to know and understand what the family system was before the crisis. The parish minister sees the adolescent in the family in a variety of other contexts and may have a more holistic understanding of the etiology, resources, and potentials of a crisis. This unique situation helps particularly in dealing with identity and addiction issues. Veteran substance-abuse counselors are increasingly turning to a family systems approach as the basis of their interventions with teenagers.[2] Knowing the family and the history of the family in the parish can be very important when the minister works with others on a crisis response team in the community setting.

The biblical imperative to minister to the "least of these" must include adolescents. By the nature of their call, ministers accept responsibility to minister to all persons regardless of social position, race, or age. Only by excluding teenagers from the status of persons can a minister dare neglect them.

Ministers are trained in issues that arise in the contemporary adolescents' crisis. While some ministers may lack specific training in depth counseling and crisis intervention, they study issues such as the meaning and purpose of life, grief, death, and divorce. Ministers who trust their **training in biblical and theological foundations** can assist adolescents to interpret the crisis and offer hope. Furthermore, ministers are able to deal with the important issues of forgiveness and peacemaking in the family context. In most crises there is likely to be explicit or implicit blaming that can lead to long-term broken relationships. Because of the minister's understanding of the dynamics of forgiveness, reconciliation, and bonding in the community of faith, she or he can best respond to those issues.

Ministers need to get involved because they have a **ready-made peer group** to offer as a network of support for adolescents in crisis: the church youth group and the adults in the congregation who work with them are available to support and respond to the teenager in trouble. Because of the minister's relationship to these persons, she or he can orchestrate the construction of a support system in ways that a counselor or a community psychologist might find difficult, if not impossible.

Another reason for the church to become involved is that the church has an **existing youth education program** and can address crisis issues easily. Religious instruction programs are a logical place to teach sex education, respond to alcohol and drugs, and provide information on AIDS and other diseases, as well as to deal with the broader social issues of any community. The pastor and the church should already be addressing key social issues from the pulpit.

Furthermore, **the church is involved with other commu-**

nity agencies in activities that call for a response to adolescents in crisis. The minister can attend plays, concerts, and sports events to get a feel for the pressures on adolescents in a given community. She or he can go to the city council, the school board, and the media to ask for resources for adolescents. In urging parents and local leaders to develop comprehensive programs for responding to adolescents in crisis, the minister plays the role of change agent in the community.

Usually more **unused space** exists during the week in church facilities than in any other institution. Because of the accessibility of space, churches can help in providing weekday services to young people at a reduced cost in most communities.

Pastoral Care and Counseling Programs

My questionnaire asked for a list of important pastoral care issues from the ministers' perspective. While a large percentage mentioned traditional youth program functions designed to meet the developmental needs of youth on a daily basis, several did address pastoral care and counseling issues and attitudes important for working with adolescents in crisis. After discussing some of the attitudes that surfaced most frequently, we will summarize a few notable pastoral care and counseling approaches.

Attitudes for Pastoral Care with Youth

Being nonjudgmental and accepting adolescents as persons in process, not finished products, was the most frequently mentioned concept on the survey. Those who explained further were careful to distinguish a nonjudgmental attitude from valuelessness and an "anything goes" mentality. Perhaps this was best captured in the words of the fifteen-year-old who said of her minister in a follow-up interview, "She's easy for me to talk with. It's not that she accepts the stuff I do; it's that she makes me feel like I can do better. She's not always just getting on my case, but still points me in the right direction."

One pastor wrote that he found acceptance and forgiveness in relationship to teenage pregnancies were particularly significant in ministering with adolescents in crisis. One church not only accepted one young mother-to-be but interpreted to the congregation the need to continue to accept her and her child with grace and love. She has now finished college and speaks to groups about the need for ministry to other pregnant adolescents.

Being available seemed significant to a number of the respondents: "Being there when they need you," "Being on call," "Being available at various times during the day." While "one hundred percent availability" is an illusion for any professional, creating the perception of being interested in and willing to respond outside of fixed appointment times is important to adolescents. Communicating one's availability is as much of an attitude as a behavior. Nevertheless, promising and not being available is always unacceptable. Setting specific times for appointments and communicating one's availability should a crisis arise seemed to help many teens. As a symbol of availability, a few ministers give teenagers a phone number to carry in their purse or billfold in case they are ever in a serious crisis.

Adolescents interviewed during this survey confirm what many adults thought. Adolescents want someone who is **willing to listen**. One minister cautioned that we must "be open to hear them out before we begin responding." Another pointed out that it is important to let them speak for themselves. Adolescents frequently complain about teachers or parents who answer questions for them. Listening is more than passive silence. Paying attention to a person in a caring, focused way is an important part of communicating the willingness to listen. Those who have not been through a training course will perhaps be helped by materials like Gerard Egan's *The Skilled Helper*. Listening to teens means being willing to see their view of the crisis. As one listens, being nonjudgmental means not accusing them falsely. Being willing to assist them in finding forgiveness when they are at fault indicates a deeper level of hearing. The attitude of the father of the prodigal is quite important for those who listen intently to adolescents in crisis.

Knowing the adolescents' world, another significant attitude suggested by the respondents, included comments about understanding their developmental needs but focused on knowing their space-age world. To understand their relationship to computers, videos, and electronic music is an important part of comprehending their scene and understanding their symbols. Several ministers mentioned a need to be involved in the adolescents' world by attending school functions in the community and being a part of their recreational events and music concerts. While knowing the adolescents' world is important, one must remember that not all young people are alike and they must be known as individuals. Respecting individual differences and appreciating the values of individual cliques is a must.

Respecting their ideas and affirming their unique gifts is an important dynamic mentioned by several of the ministers. Assisting teenagers in discovering and calling out their giftedness is strengthened by respecting their ideas. Obviously, this means avoiding put-downs and arguments over their way of seeing the world. Lead them to self-discovery by looking at the evidence around them. Encourage them to take risks in sharing their dreams, but stay realistic. Dreaming with them about potentialities reinforces their hope for the future, but pursuing unrealistic fantasies brings problems.

Social Programs That Reflect Care

Several churches mentioned social programs designed to assist adolescents in crisis such as permitting them to do service hours when referred by the juvenile court system. One church in Florida reported that they have a residential treatment program for adolescent girls and boys whose parents want to seek help before the children enter the formal court process. For most it was a means of prevention, but for a few it was the initial stage of legal intervention. The treatment program is based on a contract between the adolescent and cottage parents where responsibilities and freedoms are very closely tied at work and school.

Another program that deserves special mention is the "one church, one child program" for minority recruitment adoptions. The simple but effective idea is to have at least one family per church adopt a child with special needs. George H. Clements, a black Roman Catholic pastor, instituted the program in Chicago in 1981 in order to help cut the backlog of children awaiting adoption there. In seven years the backlog dropped from 700 to 40 children waiting to be placed. The program has now spread to twenty-six states, where it is sponsored not only by local churches but by state urban leagues and departments of human resources. Clements, pastor of Holy Angels Roman Catholic Church on Chicago's South Side, has become involved by adopting a child himself. While such ambitious programs go beyond pastoral care interventions, they do show the need for a wide range of responses to adolescents with multiple crises.

Pastoral Care Responses That Work

A number of creative and innovative pastoral care programs were mentioned by respondents to the questionnaire. While it is impossible to discuss them all and not pertinent to identify specific locations, several concepts deserve attention. These are offered not as conclusive models but as thought generators to be taken and integrated into one's own setting.

Three types of pastoral care responses predominated: ministry through (1) support groups for persons with special needs, (2) pastoral care approaches to individuals, and (3) specialized worship experiences designed for young people. Perhaps because of demands on teenagers and time limitations of the ministers, pastoral care to adolescents in groups was mentioned most often.

Groups

While some ministers attempt to use the ongoing organizations and classes in their congregations, the youth programs most discussed were specialized ones such as retreats, seminars, and support groups.

Retreats for special groups of adolescents are an annual part of the program at some churches. These retreats become rituals for a variety of youth experiences. While some churches have retreats for all who have just turned thirteen, others have a retreat for high school seniors. Agendas on the retreats vary widely; however, most include some input in the form of letters or taped messages from the parents. The retreat formats are as varied as the congregations who plan them and reflect many unique styles. Retreats give teenagers an opportunity to be away from the pressures of home and help break down their defenses against seeking help. Adolescents discover that they are not alone in their stress and that other teens can support and care for them. A major factor in the success of the group experience is seeing other teenagers dealing with similar issues.

One variation of the group experience is a **wilderness canoe trip** for eight days, during which time the ministers conduct special programs in the evenings. One evening might be designed to dealing with drugs, another with alcohol, another with sex, another with peer pressure, another with parents, and so forth. The bonding from each day's adventures can be a powerful force for growth. Experiences such as retreats provide opportunities for adolescents to be away from their parents and to form mentor relationships with trustworthy, caring professionals while discussing concerns with their peers.

Another group experience, a **weekly coffeehouse**, was much more popular during the 1960s and 1970s but still survives in some places. One church in Florida is particularly successful in bringing adolescents off the street into a Wednesday night program where frank and honest discussions about drugs and sex are regular menu items. The need to seek help is a standard part of the interchanges. The ministry of confrontation is as useful as the ministry of support and reconciliation. It seems that much of the success of this program depends on a young adult leader who himself was part of the drug culture before becoming a Christian. The peer pressure in that particular group is toward growth, getting off drugs, and finding help for oneself in the context of a loving community.

Care groups that meet on a weekly or monthly basis are part of the pastoral care program of several churches. The groups vary from the task of information-giving to a format near therapy where individuals present a particular case (or even tell of their own struggles) and find support in the group's discussion. Care groups are successful when trained adult leaders can stay involved over a sustained period of time. Confidentiality contracts are a must in groups that involve the sharing of personal information. Trust in the leader's ability to handle the traumas mentioned often determines the level of sharing. One church conducts a regular prayer meeting for young persons that combines elements of care, support group, and worship. The topics around the care groups vary widely and include such things as school problems, grief, conflict with parents, alcohol, drugs, sex, AIDS, cults, and satanic worship.

Seminars on special-interest topics designed to meet primarily for a weekend or an extended evening have many of the elements of the care group but differ in time and context. While several of the seminars bring small churches together, others reflect an ecumenical nature, with a few larger churches participating. Usually the seminars involve films or outside speakers; however, some are conducted by skilled lay-persons and professionals within the congregation. Like the care groups, the special seminars focus on a wide variety of topics. Frequently the focus is determined by a recent crisis in the church; for example, a grief seminar focused concern for the accidental death of a teenager at a swim party.

Some seminars involve creative learning activities with role plays, psychodramas, and creative art. For instance, one teacher asked her group during a seminar on identity to take a brown paper bag and build a two-sided collage. On the outside of the bag teenagers were asked to paste pictures from magazines that showed how they thought the rest of the world viewed them. Pictures of clothes, entertainment, cars, and other identity symbols dominated the exterior of the bags. Inside the bag the teens were asked to collect pictures of what they knew about themselves that the rest of the group did not know. This could include private struggles, personal accomplishment, family agendas, or other items. In the group discussion time that followed, each adolescent was given an opportunity to describe the exterior of the created art piece and then take pictures from the inside, discuss them briefly, and ask for group response.

In addition to the group responses for youth in general, a couple of churches mentioned **special needs groups** for adolescents in their congregation. For example, one church had a group that discussed the special needs of young people with disabilities, a group that included those with handicaps and those without. Another minister described a unique group designed to facilitate the understanding of the pressures between the racial groups in the community. These focused groups were usually of a short-term nature and focused on a specific topic. One minister had a group for teenagers who were contemplating marriage. In another group discussing preparation for marriage, teenagers were permitted to ask questions of couples who had been married ten, twenty, thirty, and forty years. A pre- and post-testing of these teenagers revealed significant growth in understanding the roles and the nature of Christian marriage.

Individuals

In addition to the group pastoral care responses, a number of responses reflect the flexibility needed to minister with adolescents as individuals in crisis. These demonstrate high degrees of initiative on the ministers' part.

One minister invites each troubled teenager into the parsonage for a meal and a discussion of the crisis he or she has just experienced. He reports that the young people respond very positively to being in his home and take much more initiative in seeking help after the informal **in-home experience**. While the agenda for dealing with the crisis is quite formal, the context offers warmth and informality. Obviously, individual ministry with young people in crisis is greatly enhanced any time the pastor has a positive relationship before the crisis occurs. However, even on an introductory basis, inviting adolescents into the minister's home can be a powerful symbol of acceptance and support.

A number of respondents discussed individual **visitation patterns** and offered suggestions. One pastor urges others to go visit as soon as the crisis comes to their attention. Another always follows up the initial visit with a series of phone calls (and, when needed, a referral for professional help). Visiting the hospital is a significant part of the ministry of many of the respondents. While the need for hospital ministry for adolescents was seen as very low—these youngsters are hospitalized infrequently—74 percent of those responding said they had visited a teenager in the hospital as a regular part of their ministry.

One unique approach to hospital visitation by a church in Hawaii is to take a group of teenagers along with the pastor (or youth minister) to sing for hospitalized patients. Because this program had been going on for a number of years, frequently the hospital will call with a request that the youth group come to sing for a particular patient. Members of this church felt that the patient found great meaning in receiving the attention and support, but that the youngsters who participated by singing and visiting were equally energized.

Another individual's response to crisis is a church-sponsored twenty-four-hour **crisis hotline**. The church trains its own members to take the calls. When the hotline cannot be dealt with personally, an answering machine assures callers of a returned call early in the morning. A paid professional counselor reviews the tapes each morning and responds to the adolescents in crisis.

Worship

Worship experiences that focus particularly on the needs of adolescents in crisis were mentioned by several respondents. Worship addresses some needs explicitly and meets others implicitly.

Pastoral care needs can be addressed regularly in **sermons**. One minister said, "Don't be afraid to preach to their needs." Another pastor revealed that in every sermon he tries to include at least one illustration that will address a developmental or emergency crisis of adolescents. He went on to add that he attempts to include an illustration for each developmental group in the congregation somewhere during his sermon.

Special attention was paid to meeting the needs of individuals through the **funerals** of young persons. Conducting the funeral of a youth is particularly traumatic; however, it provides an opportunity for grief ministry and for building relationships that can be followed up after the funeral. Many times, after the funeral of a young person, rituals will erupt from within the youth community as continued attempts to grapple with the grief and confusion. For example, after a particularly gruesome automobile accident, teenagers brought flowers to the scene of the accident for a number of weeks afterward. They were searching for an expression of their grief.

Religious music concerts were mentioned as a way of helping youth express pent-up feelings. Also these aid in building a positive sense of community identity. Young people like to belong to a group that stands for "goodness" and "has fun," replied one youth minister.

Counseling Resources

A wide variety of pastoral resources were mentioned as useful in dealing with counseling adolescents. As we turn our attention to a discussion of these, we will deal primarily with those not mentioned in previous chapters.

Counseling experiences with adolescents in crisis vary from informal conversations with the minister conducted at youth fellowships to formal pastoral psychotherapy conducted in church-based pastoral counseling centers. The format for offering professional pastoral counseling varies only slightly, while the approach to the counseling by both specialists and generalists varies widely. The format of professional pastoral counseling revealed in the survey focuses primarily on church-based and hospital-based programs. One clinical pastoral education training program provides free counseling for older teenagers and young adults as a part of the training program for their pastoral interns. On the other hand, several churches responded that they have professional pastoral counseling centers in the church or use freestanding pastoral counseling centers sponsored by a denominational or ecumenical group within the community. One church reported that they employ a part-time pastoral counselor to work only with teenagers and their families.

Ministers who are not trained counselors discuss crises informally while participating in youth activities. They hold crisis ministry conversations such as visiting young people in the hospital or mental health facility. However, they tend to avoid regular counseling sessions.

Formal pastoral counseling seems to focus in three areas: family counseling, group counseling, and vocational counseling. Very little was said to distinguish between these approaches to adolescents and the routine methods used in adult counseling. Several persons did mention that in family counseling they try to avoid stereotyping the adolescent as the identified patient and to work with the unit as a whole.

One group does provide psychological testing at the church. This includes primarily vocational testing, but personality inventory testing is included in making referrals.

By way of summary, it appears that a wide variety of individual and group responses to the needs of adolescents effectively minister in some locations. Teens vary significantly. While some appear arrogant, proud, and defiant, others are confident, caring, and involved. Still others are hurt, scared, detached, and suffering. However, enough similarities exist for churches to plan programs to meet their needs. Ongoing activities reach most young people, but special, focused pastoral care and counseling approaches are needed for those for whom a major change brings danger, not opportunity. Teens who have a supportive family and who find a caring professional to shepherd them through a time of crisis can return to their everyday tasks and to normal development. Those whose initial emergencies go untended follow a path of continued troubles and increased dysfunction. Ignored crises escalate and expand.

Being a shepherd with adolescents in crisis is an awesome

responsibility. Get all of the help you can. Do not overestimate your abilities, and don't try to do too much alone. Get involved in a consultation group, find supervision with professionals, and join interdisciplinary case conferences whenever possible. As you guide one youngster into adulthood, rejoice briefly and then turn to the next child struggling with the crises of adolescence.

Notes

Chapter 1: Adolescents in Crisis

1. *Miami Herald,* December 5, 1987, section B, p. 1.
2. The Eli Lilly Foundation Project at 3401 Brook Road, Union Theological Seminary in Virginia, Richmond, VA 23227, has information on examples of an ongoing study of youth ministry programs.
3. Wayne E. Oates, *New Dimensions in Pastoral Care* (Philadelphia: Fortress Press, 1970).
4. David D. Burns, *Feeling Good: The New Mood Therapy* (New York: Signet Books, 1981).
5. For further discussions see William A. Clebsch and Charles R. Jaekle, *Pastoral Care in Historical Perspective* (Englewood Cliffs, N.J.: Prentice-Hall, 1964), and Seward Hiltner, *Preface to Pastoral Theology.* (Full facts of publication for this work, and for others cited in the Notes, are given in the Bibliography.) Wayne Oates in *Pastoral Counseling* discusses a dynamic tension approach to several other facets of the counseling task.

Chapter 2: Developmental Issues and Crises

1. E. James Anthony, "Normal Adolescent Development from a Cognitive Viewpoint," *Journal of the American Academy of Child Psychiatry,* vol. 21 (1982), p. 318.
2. David Elkind, *All Grown Up and No Place to Go,* p. 3.
3. Derek Miller, *Adolescence,* p. 436.
4. James W. Fowler, *The Stages of Faith.*

Chapter 3: Principles of Caring

1. Wayne E. Oates, *The Christian Pastor,* 3rd ed., rev. (Philadelphia. Westminster Press, 1982), pp. 194–199.
2. James W. Fowler, *The Stages of Faith,* pp. 151–173 .
3. Ibid., pp. 244–245.
4. Randy James Simmons, "Content and Structure in Faith Devel-

opment," unpublished Ph.D. dissertation, Southern Baptist Theological Seminary, 1986, p. 201.

5. E. Mansell Pattison, "Religious Youth Cults: Alternative Healing Social Networks," *Journal of Religion and Health,* vol. 19, no. 4 (Fall/Winter 1980), p. 278.

Chapter 4: Methods for Pastoral Care and Counseling

1. Norman Kagan, *Interpersonal Process Recall: A Method of Influencing Human Interaction* (Copyright 1975, 1976, Norman I. Kagan).

2. Jesse H. Wright and Aaron T. Beck, "Cognitive Therapy of Depression: Theory and Practice," *Hospital and Community Psychiatry,* vol. 34, no. 12 (Dec. 1983), pp. 1119–1126.

3. G. Randolph Schrodt and Barbara A. Fitzgerald, "Cognitive Therapy with Adolescents," *American Journal of Psychotherapy,* vol. 41, no. 3 (July 1987), pp. 402–408.

4. Wright and Beck, p. 1119.

5. For a detailed discussion of cognitive errors see David D. Burns, *Feeling Good: The New Mood Therapy* (New York: Signet Books, 1981).

6. Schrodt and Fitzgerald, pp. 407–408.

7. Wright and Beck, pp. 1119–1120.

8. Marsha P. Mirkin and Stuart L. Koman, eds., *Handbook of Adolescents and Family Therapy,* p. 3.

9. See James C. Hansen and Lucinano L'Abate, *Approaches to Family Therapy* (New York: Macmillan Publishing Co., 1982), p. 121.

10. Ibid., p. 52.

11. Ibid., p. 171.

12. Eric Berne, *Games People Play: The Psychology of Human Relationships* (New York: Grove Press, 1964).

13. Thomas C. Oden, *Game Free: A Guide to the Meaning of Intimacy* (San Francisco: Harper & Row, 1974).

14. E. Mansell Pattison, "Religious Youth Cults: Alternative Healing Social Networks," *Journal of Religion and Health,* vol. 19, no. 4 (Fall/Winter 1980), p. 277.

15. Edgar Draper et al., "On the Diagnostic Values of Religious Ideation," *Archives of General Psychiatry,* vol. 13 (Sept. 1965), pp. 202–207.

Chapter 5: Family Problems

1. Nathan W. Ackerman, *The Psychodynamics of Family Living* (New York: Basic Books, 1972).

2. See Janet G. Woititz, *Adult Children of Alcoholics* (Pompano Beach, Fla.: Health Communications, 1983).

3. Daniel Offer, Eric Astrov, Kenneth I. Howard, eds., *Patterns of Adolescent Self-Image* (San Francisco: Jossey-Bass, 1984), p. 68.

4. Merton P. Strommen, *The Five Cries of Youth,* pp. 36–37.

5. Dean Hoge, "Study of High School Seniors from Monitoring the Future 'Data,'" unpublished paper at Catholic University, 1987, p. 17.

6. Dean Hoge, "Half of Teens Are Regular Attendees of Religious Services," *Emerging Trends,* Princeton Religious Research Center, vol. 10, no. 3 (March 1988), p. 2.

7. Randy James Simmons, "Content and Structure in Faith Development," unpublished Ph.D. dissertation, Southern Baptist Theological Seminary, 1986, pp. 207–209.

8. For a complete discussion of the dynamics of parenting in a two-career context, see G. Wade Rowatt, Jr., and Mary Jo Brock Rowatt, *The Two-Career Marriage,* pp. 41–57.

Chapter 6: Sexual Problems

1. David R. Mace, *The Christian Response to the Sexual Revolution* (Nashville: Abingdon Press, 1970); William Graham Cole, *Sex and Love in the Bible* (New York: Association Press, 1959).

2. John W. Whitehead, "Pregnant and Unmarried," in Jay Kesler, ed., *Parents and Teenagers,* p. 505.

3. J. Patrick LaVery et al., "Pregnancy Outcome in a Comprehensive Teenage Parent Program," *Adolescent Pediatric Gynecology,* vol. 1 (1988), p. 34.

4. Ibid., p. 36.

5. "Rehearsal Follows Moms 17 Years Later," *Newsletter of the Colorado Organization of Adolescent Pregnancy and Parenting,* Dec 1987, p. 1.

6. Whitehead, pp. 506–507.

7. David Rolfe, "Pastoral Opportunities to Help Families Prevent Teenage Pregnancy," *Journal of Pastoral Care,* vol. 38 (March 1984), p. 31.

8. "Rehearsal Follows Moms . . . ," p. 1.

9. Marsha P. Mirkin and Stuart L. Koman, eds., *Handbook of Adolescents and Family Therapy,* p. 32.

10. Derek Miller, *Adolescence,* pp. 428, 429.

11. Judith Marks Mishne, *Clinical Work with Adolescents,* pp. 261, 278.

12. Ibid., p. 281.

13. Derek Miller, *Adolescence,* p. 428.

14. Mishne, *Clinical Work with Adolescents,* p. 276.

15. Derek Miller, *Adolescence,* p. 406.

Chapter 7: Peer and Academic Pressures

1. Charlotte Dickson Moore, ed., *Science Reports: Adolescence and Stress,* p. 76.

2. Ibid., p. 76.

3. Merton P. Strommen, *The Five Cries of Youth,* pp. 118–121.

4. Moore, *Science Reports,* p. 75.

5. Ibid.

6. E. Mansell Patterson, "Religious Youth Cults: Alternative Healing Social Networks," *Journal of Religion and Health,* vol. 19, no. 4 (Fall/Winter 1980), pp. 275–284.

7. Group for the Advancement of Psychiatry, *Normal Adolescence* (New York: Charles Scribner's Sons, 1969), p. 68, and Judith Marks Mishne, *Clinical Work with Adolescents,* p. 12.

8. Strommen, *Five Cries of Youth,* p. 29.

9. Ibid., p. 78.

10. Kathleen Stassen Berger, *The Developing Person Through the Life Span,* 2nd ed. (New York: Worth Publishers, 1988), p. 370.

11. Strommen, *Five Cries of Youth,* p. 32.

12. Mishne, *Clinical Work with Adolescents,* p. 167.

13. Moore, *Science Reports,* p. 82.

14. For a full discussion of this program read Thomas Gordon, *Teacher Effectiveness Training* (New York: David McKay Co., 1975).

15. Derek Miller, *Adolescence,* p. 121.

Chapter 8: Depression and Suicide

1. Judith Marks Mishne, *Clinical Work with Adolescents,* p. 147.

2. For further information see G. Randolph Schrodt and Barbara A. Fitzgerald, "Cognitive Therapy with Adolescents," *American Journal of Psychotherapy,* vol. 41, no. 3 (July 1987), pp. 402–408; and Jesse H. Wright, "Cognitive Therapy of Depression," *American Psychiatric Press Review of Psychiatry,* vol. 7 (1988); and Jesse H. Wright and Aaron T. Beck, "Cognitive Therapy of Depression: Theory and Practice," *Hospital and Community Psychiatry,* vol. 34, no. 12 (Dec. 1983), p. 1119.

3. Jerry Johnson, *Why Suicide?* (Nashville: Thomas Nelson Publishers, 1987), pp. 10–11.

4. Ibid., p. 17.

5. Ibid., p. 133.

6. Marsha P. Mirkin and Stuart L. Koman, eds., *Handbook of Adolescents and Family Therapy,* p. 310.

7. Ibid., p. 10.

8. Ibid., p. 310.

9. William Van Ornum and John B. Mordock, *Crisis Counseling with Children and Adolescents,* p. 80.

Chapter 9: Substance Abuse

1. Mia Adessa, "Coke Isn't It," *Psychology Today,* May 1988, p. 16.

2. Carla M. Felsted, ed., *Youth and Alcohol Abuse: Readings and Resources* (Phoenix: Oryx Press, 1986), p. 15.

3. Richard D. Parsons, *Adolescents in Turmoil, Parents Under Stress,* p. 87.

4. Derek Miller, *Adolescence,* p. 442.

5. Gina Kolata, "Alcoholic Genes or Misbehavior," *Psychology Today,* May 1968, p. 36.

6. Ibid.

7. Judith Marks Mishne, *Clinical Work with Adolescents,* p. 238.

8. For further discussion see Fariborz Amini, Sheil Salasnek, and Edward L. Burke, "Adolescent Drug Use: Etiological and Treatment Considerations," *Adolescents,* vol. 11, no. 42 (Summer 1976), pp. 281–299.

9. Henry Wechsler and Mary McFadden, "Sex Differences in Adolescent Alcohol and Drug Use, a Disappearing Phenomenon," *Journal of Statistics on Alcohol,* vol. 37, no. 9 (1976), pp. 1291–1301.

10. See Fariborz Amini, Nathan Zilberg, Edward L. Burke, and Sheil Salasnek, "A Controlled Study of Inpatient vs. Outpatient Treatment of Delinquent Drug Abusing Adolescents: One Year Results," *Comprehensive Psychiatry,* vol. 23, no. 5 (Sept./Oct., 1982), p. 436.

11. Derek Miller, *Adolescence,* p. 496.

12. Paul E. Garfinkel and David M. Garner, *Anorexia Nervosa: A Multidimensional Perspective* (New York: Brunner/Mazel, 1982), p. 276.

13. Thomas C. Todd, "Anorexia Nervosa and Bulimia," in Marsha P. Mirkin and Stuart L. Koman, eds., *Handbook of Adolescents and Family Therapy,* p. 235.

14. Garfinkel and Garner, *Anorexia Nervosa,* p. 261.

15. Ibid., p. 263.

16. Ibid., pp. 285–288.

Chapter 10: The Churches Respond

1. "Kudzu," *Atlanta Journal,* Sept. 1982, p. 4B.

2. James Fulton, Jr., "Intervention with Adolescents," *Professional Counselor,* Nov./Dec. 1987, p. 14.

Bibliography

Ackerman, Norman J. *A Theory of Family Systems*. New York: Gardner Press, 1984.

Aleshire, Daniel O. *Faithcare: Ministering to All God's People Through the Ages of Life*. Philadelphia: Westminster Press, 1988.

Apthorp, Stephen P. *Alcohol and Substance Abuse*. Wilton, Conn.: Morehouse-Barlow Co., 1985.

Arnold, William V. *Introduction to Pastoral Care*. Philadelphia: Westminster Press, 1982.

Augsburger, David W. *Pastoral Counseling Across Cultures*. Philadelphia: Westminster Press, 1986.

Barnes, Jr., Robert G. *Confident Kids*. Wheaton, Ill.: Tyndale House Publishers, 1987.

————. *Single Parenting*. Wheaton, Ill.: Tyndale House Publishers, 1987.

Blackburn, Bill. *Caring in Times of Family Crisis*. Nashville: Convention Press, 1987.

Bolton, Iris. *My Son, My Son*. Atlanta: Bolton Press, 1983.

Borchert, Gerald L., and Andrew D. Lester, eds. *Spiritual Dimensions of Pastoral Care: Witness to the Ministry of Wayne E. Oates*. Philadelphia: Westminster Press, 1985.

Brister, C. W. *Pastoral Care in the Church*. New York: Harper & Row, 1977.

Bugental, James F. T. *The Art of the Psychotherapist*. New York: W. W. Norton & Co., 1987.

Capps, Donald. *Biblical Approaches to Pastoral Counseling*. Philadelphia: Westminster Press, 1981.

————. *Deadly Sin and Saving Virtues*. Philadelphia: Fortress Press, 1987.

Clinebell, Howard M., Jr. *Basic Types of Pastoral Care and Counseling: Resource for the Minister of Healing and Growth*. Rev. & enl. ed. Nashville: Abingdon Press, 1984.

————. *Contemporary Growth Therapies*. Nashville: Abingdon Press, 1981.

————. *Understanding and Counseling the Alcoholic.* Nashville: Abingdon Press, 1985.

Corey, Gerald F., and Marianne Schneider Corey. *Groups: Process and Practice.* 2nd ed. Monterey, Calif.: Brooks/Cole Publishing Co., 1982.

Deutsch, Helene. *Selected Problems of Adolescence.* New York: International Universities Press, 1967.

Duvall, Evelyn. *Handbook for Parents.* Nashville: Broadman Press, 1974.

Egan, Gerard. *The Skilled Helper: A Systematic Approach to Effective Helping.* 3rd ed. Monterey, Calif.: Brooks/Cole Publishing Co., 1986.

Elkind, David. *All Grown Up and No Place to Go: Teenagers in Crisis.* Reading, Mass.: Addison-Wesley Publishing Co., 1984.

Emmett, Steven Willey, ed. *Theory and Treatment of Anorexia Nervosa and Bulimia.* New York: Brunner/Mazel, 1985.

Feindler, Eva L., and Randolph B. Ecton. *Adolescent Anger Control.* Elmsford, N.Y.: Pergamon Press, 1986.

Fowler, James W. *The Stages of Faith: The Psychology of Human Development and the Quest for Meaning.* New York: Harper & Row, 1981.

Friedman, Edwin H. *Generation to Generation.* New York: Guilford Press, 1985.

Gallatin, Judith E. *Adolescence and Individuality.* New York: Harper & Row, 1975.

Gerkin, Charles V. *The Living Human Document.* Nashville: Abingdon Press, 1984.

Gilligan, Carol. *In a Different Voice: Psychological Theory and Women's Development.* Cambridge, Mass.: Harvard University Press, 1982.

Glasser, William. *Stations of the Mind: New Directions for Reality Therapy.* New York: Harper & Row, 1981.

Grant, Wayne W. *Growing Children.* Nashville: Convention Press, 1977.

Herring, Reuben. *Becoming Friends with Your Children.* Nashville: Broadman Press, 1984.

Hiltner, Seward. *Preface to Pastoral Theology.* Nashville: Abingdon Press, 1958.

————. *Theological Dynamics.* Nashville: Abingdon Press, 1972.

Husain, Syed Arshad. *Suicide in Children and Adolescents.* Jamaica, N.Y.: Spectrum Publications, 1984.

Kemp, Charles F. *The Caring Pastor.* Nashville: Abingdon Press, 1985.

————. *Physicians of the Soul.* New York: Macmillan Co., 1947.

Kesler, Jay, ed., with Ronald A. Beers. *Parents and Teenagers.* Wheaton, Ill.: Victor Books, 1984.

Lester, Andrew D. *Pastoral Care with Children in Crisis.* Philadelphia: Westminster Press, 1985.

————. *Sex Is More Than a Word.* Nashville: Broadman Press, 1973.

Lovinger, Robert J. *Working with Religious Issues in Therapy.* New York: Jason Aronson, 1984.

May, Rollo. *The Meaning of Anxiety.* New York: W. W. Norton & Co., 1977.

Mayeroff, Milton. *On Caring.* New York: Harper & Row, 1971.

Mickey, Paul, and Gary Gamble. *Pastoral Assertiveness.* Nashville: Abingdon Press, 1978.

Miller, Alice. *For Your Own Good: Hidden Cruelty in Child-rearing and the Roots of Violence.* New York: Farrar, Straus & Giroux, 1983.

Miller, Derek. *Adolescence: Psychology, Psychopathology, and Psychotherapy.* New York: Jason Aronson, 1974.

————. *Attack on the Self: Adolescent Behavioral Disturbances and Their Treatment.* New York: Jason Aronson, 1986.

Mirkin, Marsha P., and Stuart L. Koman, eds. *Handbook of Adolescents and Family Therapy.* New York: Gardner Press, 1985.

Mishne, Judith Marks. *Clinical Work with Adolescents.* New York: Free Press, 1986.

Moore, Charlotte Dickson, ed. *Science Reports: Adolescence and Stress.* Washington, D.C.: U.S. Department of Health and Human Services, 1981.

Nutt, Grady. *Being Me.* Nashville: Broadman Press, 1971.

Oates, Wayne E. *Behind the Masks: Personality Disorders in Religious Behavior.* Philadelphia: Westminster Press, 1987.

————. *The Bible in Pastoral Care.* Grand Rapids: Baker Book House, 1973.

————. *Christ and Selfhood.* New York: Association Press, 1961.

————. *On Becoming Children of God.* Philadelphia: Westminster Press, 1969.

————. *Pastoral Counseling.* Philadelphia: Westminster Press, 1974.

Oettinger, Katherine B. *Normal Adolescence: Its Dynamics and Impact.* New York: Charles Scribner's Sons, 1968.

Parke, Ross D. *The Family.* Chicago: University of Chicago Press, 1984.

Parsons, Richard D. *Adolescents in Turmoil, Parents Under Stress: A Pastoral Ministry Primer.* New York: Paulist Press, 1987.

Patton, John. *Pastoral Counseling: A Ministry of the Church.* Nashville: Abingdon Press, 1983.

Pruyser, Paul W. *The Minister as Diagnostician: Personal Problems in Pastoral Perspective.* Philadelphia: Westminster Press, 1976.

Ross, Richard, and G. Wade Rowatt, Jr. *Ministry with Youth and Their Parents.* Nashville: Convention Press, 1986.

Rowatt, G. Wade, Jr., and Mary Jo Brock Rowatt. *The Two-Career Marriage.* Christian Care Books. Philadelphia: Westminster Press, 1980.

Shelp, Earl E., and Ronald H. Sunderland. *AIDS and the Church.* Philadelphia: Westminster Press, 1987.

Sherrill, Lewis Joseph. *The Struggle of the Soul.* New York: Macmillan Co., 1951.

Stone, Howard W. *Crisis Counseling.* Philadelphia: Fortress Press, 1978.

————. *Using Behavioral Methods in Pastoral Counseling.* Philadelphia: Fortress Press, 1980.

Strommen, Merton P. *The Five Cries of Youth.* New York: Harper & Row, 1974.

Switzer, David K. *The Minister as a Crisis Counselor.* Nashville: Abingdon Press, 1974.

Thornton, Edward E. *Being Transformed: An Inner Way of Spiritual Growth.* Philadelphia: Westminster Press, 1984.

Van Ornum, William, and John B. Mordock. *Crisis Counseling with Children and Adolescents.* New York: Continuum Publishing Co., 1983.

Waterman, Alan S., ed. *Identity in Adolescence: Processes and Content.* San Francisco: Jossey-Bass, 1985.

Weeks, Louis. *Making Ethical Decisions: A Casebook.* Philadelphia: Westminster Press, 1987.

White, Ernest. *The Art of Human Relations.* Nashville: Broadman Press, 1985.

Wicks, Robert, Richard Parsons, and Donald Capps, eds. *Clinical Handbook of Pastoral Counseling.* New York: Paulist Press, 1984.

Wynn, J. C. *Family Therapy in Pastoral Ministry.* San Francisco: Harper & Row, 1982.